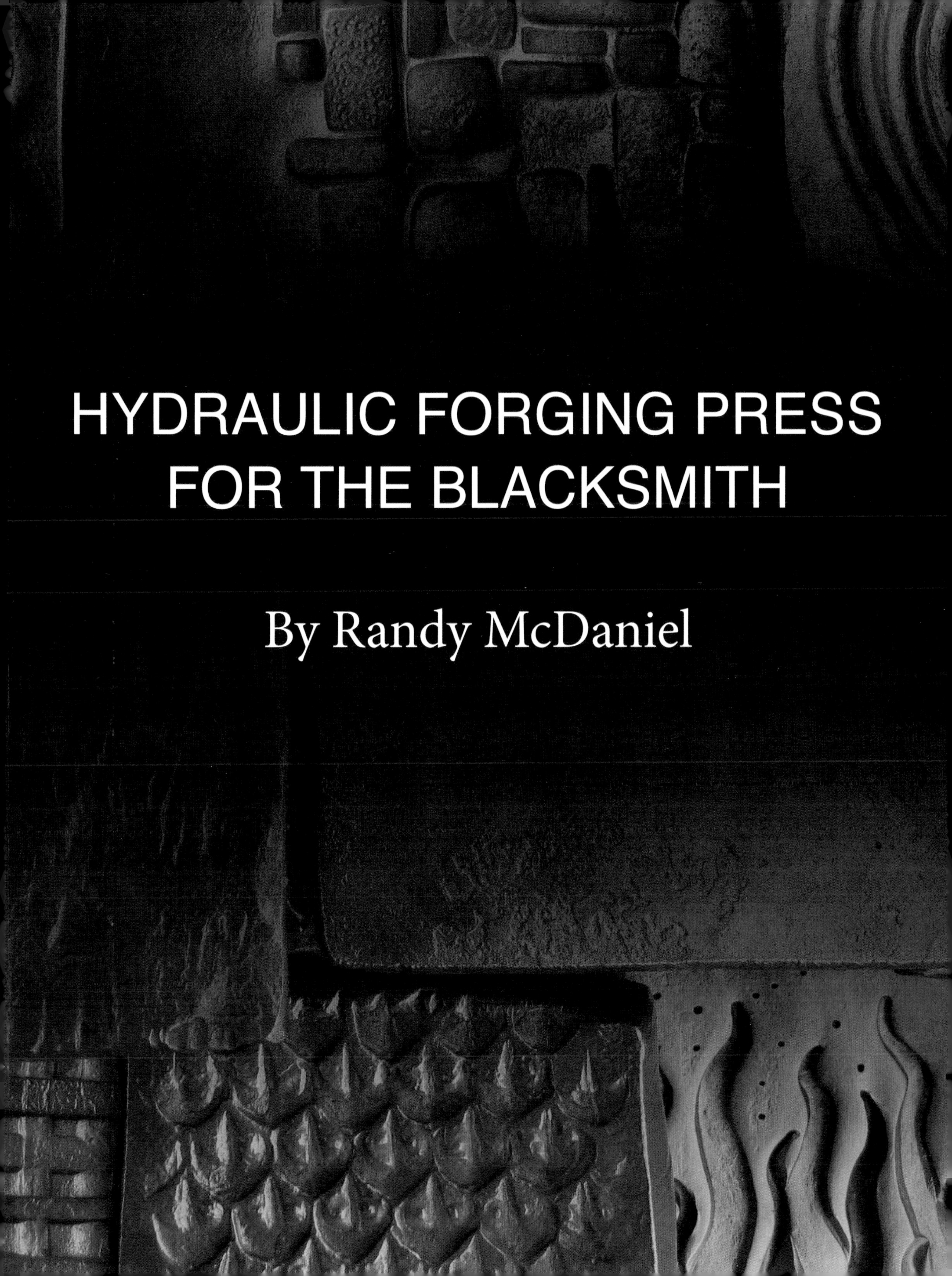

HYDRAULIC FORGING PRESS FOR THE BLACKSMITH

By Randy McDaniel

Hard Cover ISBN: 978-1-879535-29-9

Production Notes
Unless otherwise stated all photos were taken and all drawings were done by and are copyright © Randy McDaniel.
Cover Photo: Author, Randy McDaniel with his 60 ton hydraulic forging press
Cover and Layout Design: Sonya Boushek
Indexed: Dianna Haught, words by Haught
Publisher: Alan E. Krysan

SkipJack Press
An Imprint of Finney Company

5995 149th Street West, Suite 105
Apple Valley, Minnesota 55124
www.finneyco.com • www.astragalpress.com

Printed in the United States of America

Dedication

This book is dedicated to all of the smiths who have guided me down my path in forging hot metals and to the future smiths whose job it will be to carry on the legacy and to pass it on to the following generations. Special thanks go to all of the people who have graciously shared their time and information either through technical data or through photographs to help all of us learn as much as possible about the blacksmith forging press.

Forward

This was written as an informational guide for those considering building or purchasing a hydraulic forging press for a blacksmithing or knife making operation and describes the benefits of forging hot metal and working some metal cold. I say "metal" as it could be steel, wrought iron, a pattern welded billet, stainless steel, bronze, copper or even titanium. In most instances I do not like how the press works with aluminum except working it cold. There is no heat color in aluminum to determine how hot it is and as the dies or tooling pull heat from the bar you have nothing to use as a guide to tell if it is safe to work or not.

This book will explain the different characteristics and operations of the forging press in order to help you decide what type of press will work best for you. It will not tell you how to build one. I am not a designer of presses. Others can help you better with designs and builds, but understanding about presses will help in your build or choice of which one to buy. I will focus on the presses made for the blacksmith/metalworking shop, not the industrial shop. It will describe many ways this is a beneficial tool to have in your shop and the type of tooling to have to get the most out of your press. This is written for someone who has some knowledge of forging hot metal, not for a novice!

I have collected this information from working with my press since 2006, from information I have researched and from fellow smiths who have been gracious enough to share what they have learned with me. Thank you to all who have assisted me in this endeavor!

Table of Contents

Important Statements to Know and Understand Before We Begin:

Number 1. Presses are a very dangerous machine and should be used with the utmost caution! They can incapacitate, maim or kill you or others around you! They must be used with understanding, focus and care at all times.

Number 2. This information is based on my experiences in using my own press and what I have learned over the years. Other solutions may be available.

Number 3. There may be exceptions in construction and operation, but they require putting safety first!

Number 4. It is imperative that you know as much about hand forging and heat treating before you operate a power hammer or a forging press. *Power does not ignore ignorance, it magnifies it!* The more you know about how hot metal works under a hand hammer with anvil and the basic hammer blows the better and safer these machines will be.

Number 5. Understanding heat treating is required for making your own tooling and dies, but it is also necessary for understanding what is happening to your metal when it is cooled rapidly by your dies or tooling in the press and will help you prevent metal shattering while working. If you do not have this knowledge then take some forging and tool making classes and read as much as you can about it before operating a press.

1 History of the Hydraulic Forging Press

The history of the hydraulic forging press is difficult to nail down, but there are some things that are recorded. In 1795 Joseph Bramah (1748–1814), was given a patent for his hydraulic press. He is considered as one of the fathers of hydraulic engineering. He lived in England and was an inventor and locksmith. In many places you will see a hydraulic press listed as a Braham press. Though not a forging press this is what started the ball rolling.

Now here's where it get confusing yet close to what we are looking for in regards to a time line for the forging press. There are a lot of minutes of meetings in the 1800's held by civil engineers, marine engineers, forging groups and institutions which talk about the hydraulic forging press, but they are not always specific on dates, but I think I may have it pinned down. Approximately in 1894 there was a paper written in England known as "Forging by Hydraulic Pressure" by Mr. R.H. Tweddell, which includes a brief history of the hydraulic forging press going back to 1846. In another paper in 1876 it states that 30 years earlier Sir Charles Fox patented an invention for using hydraulic presses for squeezing iron. So that also puts the beginnings of forging iron with a hydraulic press as 1846 at least in England.

The earliest record I found of actual hydraulic forging presses in use was also in England. In 1861 an 800 ton hydraulic press was used for forging locomotive parts. Also the Kirkstall Forge produced a 1,250 ton forging press in 1863. Now those were in the UK and who knows what was being done in other parts of the world. I did find that in America in 1887 the Bethlehem Iron Company installed two hydraulic forging presses, one 2,000 ton and one 5,000 ton press. That means we have over 125 years of the hydraulic forging press being used in the US!

Those are a bit big for our use, but the concept is basically the same as what we use. Most of the forging presses in blacksmith shops are from about 15 to 200 tons.

I believe that we have the forged knife makers to thank for the design and advancement in its use in the blacksmith shop today. Though blacksmith shops have been using hydraulic forging presses for the last 100 years, it was the knife makers who came up with a way to make them so that they are economical and convenient for the small shop. Forging presses are very advantageous in forging pattern welded steel and even in forging the bloom when smelting iron used in knife making. By using easily available I-beams or heavy wall tubing press frames can be made to withstand the forces created by a press. They also produced ready to use presses, press plans and even a book to put most of the information together so that anyone with good fabrication skills could build one of these powerful machines for their own shop and economically. Website forums and internet videos played a big part in spreading the word of what a press can do to a piece of hot metal so that more people saw how this machine can be an asset for the hot metal worker.

2 My Background & Journey

I have been forging hot metal since 1972. I have worked with hand hammers, strikers, mechanical hammers and air hammers. One of the things that I enjoy about hot metal forging and teaching is showing how this "lifeless" material does have life when heat and enough energy is put into it. I specially love how it works like modeling clay. Since my class with Ivan Bailey back in the 1980's I have been looking for a way to produce more of the clay looking effect in my work. I have not found anything that makes hot metal look like it was squished in my fingers more than a hydraulic forging press.

In 2002 I was invited to an old blacksmith shop outside of Reading, Pennsylvania, to see if there was anything left that I would be interested in purchasing. The smith had been gone from us for years and most everything had been auctioned off years before this visit. All of the equipment and tools were gone from this old carriage house style shop. I was able to purchase a hand forged floor lamp that was in the house that had a vine of iron flowers wrapped around it and showed me what a wonderful talent this smith had been. I found myself frustrated that I had never met him or had the chance to learn some of his skills. I still feel this way.

I looked in a box of "this and that" and found three designs that to me looked like "tiles" in wrought iron. They ranged in size from 2" to almost 4" square. They stacked up like dishes as each size was exactly alike. When I turned them over I could see the marks of hot forging and when studied on the front you could see discrepancies in the pattern on each tile. It was a sign of the hand work that went into them.

But then how were they made? They must have used hand forged dies, but what equipment could make these tiles in 1/16 inch thick steel sheet? They brought up more questions than answers. So the quest began. What could the smith that did most of his work in the 1920's to 1950's use to make these tiles? There was no sign of any special foundation for a large piece of equipment in the shop.

Forged steel "tiles" made by a blacksmith near Reading, PA

I forged out a simple textured spring die just to see what would happen in use on hot metal. I had a Nazel 1B power hammer so I tried using that on a piece of hot steel.

Randy's Nazel 1B power hammer

It was almost impossible to get just one big hit and when I got multiple hits it produced what I will call "echoes". The pattern repeated over its self with some obvious minor movement. No good. When I did one good hit it did not leave enough of an impression. He must have used a much larger hammer or another piece of equipment.

Randy's 75 pound drop hammer

I needed something that would give me one good strong hit. I had seen drop hammers so figured I would try that. I bought an eight foot, seventy-five pound drop hammer. This was not much better than the power hammer. It was too small and so it was not powerful enough to do the job. Frustrating!

Randy's kick press

While at my local scrap equipment yard I found the biggest kick press I had ever seen. Maybe this would do it? So I bought it, took it home and tried it. It still did not have enough force or power. I needed something bigger and more powerful. But what, was still the question? Meanwhile a few years have gone by with this puzzle gnawing at me. On a very good note from an economic perspective, I was able to sell the drop hammer and kick press.

I took the tiles with me when I went to blacksmith conferences and hammer-ins and not even the most experienced and talented smiths had any idea how they were made. Some guessed what I had already tried that had not worked. Most of us come from a hand and mechanical way of thinking and so were stumped.

One day I was watching a video on-line of a knife maker forging out a big pattern welded steel billet. "What was ***that*** piece of machinery? What is that you say? He built it himself?" I was excited to say the least. So now to learn more about this!

Robert Eggerling's shop circa 2006

I learned that a member of our local blacksmithing group made pattern welded/damascus steel and had a few hydraulic forging presses. "Oh, so that's what that is?" I had known him for years yet never knew exactly how he worked. I called him and made an appointment to visit him and his presses. I was amazed. Robert Eggerling is well known for his damascus steel and is a very intelligent and resourceful man. If there is something he needs to learn or something he needs to make he researches it and does it, and without a computer. I spent the whole afternoon watching him and his machines and picking his brain about the presses. At that time he had an air hammer, a small mechanical hammer and two handmade presses in his shop. When I first walked into his shop the presses were hard to see due to the lighting and the presses being the same color as the wall behind them. Soon it all came into focus and I began to better recognize and understand hydraulic forging presses.

Randy's press as first seen at Robert's shop

When the day was almost done he asked me if I would be interested in buying a press? After seeing what they could do and how this finally answered my search and dilemma, I said "definitely!" He took me down to another building where he had a frame made from a large I-beam which was already cut out and plates welded to it for strength. He had the twin cylinders reworked and all of the other parts in boxes ready to go. It still needed all of the facing, ram and anvil plates and assembly but I knew I could handle that. We came to a financial agreement and I had my press. This was not only an answer to my problem of several years, but also a new beginning for a new way of working hot metal for me.

After that day I had to get the press and mechanicals cart assembled and learn how to use this machine. Figuring out what this machine could do and what tools to use to achieve the most versatility was the next step.

3 Information to Get You Started

Usually the first question asked is: what is the difference between a power hammer and a hydraulic forging press? There are many variables between these two pieces of equipment depending on what model and size power hammer and speed and tonnage of press. There are also other machines such as the punch press and fly press to name a couple that perform similar functions. I will offer some comments and explanations on these smaller scale pieces of equipment in regards to forging hot metal.

Ed Small's 100 pound Little Giant mechanical power hammer (© EdSmall)

Matt Harris' Nazel 2B air hammer circa 1910

A **power hammer** is generally what is stated in its name. It is a hammer that uses power to push it. Whether a mechanical or air hammer it is still a hammer. So it is like your hand hammer, but with a bigger hammer head and with a power source raise it and let it drop repeatedly in a controlled direction and position. There is a weight flying down at your hot metal and hitting it to change its shape or texture. This can be one hit or a series of hits until the desired effect is achieved.

The number and speed of hammer blow repetitions is controlled by the operator. They can be used as a hammer and anvil or as hammer and tooling or dies. It is used in hot forging for drawing out, fullering, upsetting, punching holes, texturing and other operations. There are a multitude of designs and sizes of this machine. This has been the most popular piece of forging equipment in the blacksmith and knifemaker shop until recently.

Punch press at Brandywine Forge.
Ten feet high and 56 tons. (© WGreene)

A **punch press** uses inertia to get its power. A large powered flywheel spins and pushes a crankshaft up and down. You do not have the same control as a power hammer as this machine must run the full distance on each turn and then repeats the operation in a steady cadence. If something stops the progression of this cycle something will break, not only ruining the machine, but may damage the operator. It is usually used with expensive spring die sets for bending, stamping, cutting or shaping cold metal sheet. They are found from bench top models to huge industrial models. Usually this is not a good machine for forging, but some ingenious smiths have found ways to adapt it for such hot work as making repeated operations as in hot forging blacksmith tongs. This is definitely not something to mess with unless you really know what you are doing.

Steve Gensheimer fly press (© SGensheimer)

Large flypress at Baltimore Knife & Sword

A **fly press or screw press** also uses inertia with a flywheel or counter balanced weights but instead of a crankshaft it uses a screw to operate the ram. Most smiths use this as a manual operation by pulling on a handle on the flywheel or counter balanced weights. This can be used for pressing as in punching holes, coining and forging. Because of the power and hand control of this machine smiths like this for working cold or hot in order to cut in lines and decorations. It is also good for bending, making tenons and for rolling hinge eyes cold. I've even seen hammer heads made using the fly press, but they require a lot of physical energy. Many are limited by the size of material that you can put into the press. These are found as small bench top models to ones weighing several hundred tons.

Randy's 75 pound drop hammer

Drop hammers are what the name implies. They are either manual or powered in the way the hammer is raised. When it gets to the desired height the hot metal is placed in the dies and the hammer is released to drop onto the metal. Then the process is repeated. These, too, are from small hammers of say twenty pounds and pulled up by hand with a rope to ones operated by large electric motors and raising a hammer of thousands of pounds. Because of the one big hit these are usually not used in forging operations such as drawing out or open die work, but more for work between top and bottom forming dies to create a finished part such as a claw hammer head that might be made in a series of forming dies in an industry setting.

Shop presses are not good for a forging press.

Shop presses and arbor presses like you see in many catalogues are not the same machine as a forging press. They are often used for pressing in bearings in automotive shops, riveting and punching sheet metal. They do not have the speed required to be a good forging press and usually their framework would not withstand the forces put out by a forging press even though they may be of the same tonnage. Compare the frame of this type of press to a forging press. Most arbor presses are operated by a hand lever and a cam, but I have seen industrial ones that are hydraulic. Most of the shop presses use a bottle jack that you pump by hand and use springs for the return stroke instead of hydraulics powering it, but some have an air assist system to power the cylinder. Again there are exceptions to this as I have seen it used for hot forming bowls and hot bending, but I would not consider a shop press for most forging operations.

Bottle jack presses are a manually operated press, usually used by jewelers in cold work for cutting forms, pressing die work and forming small work, often in non-ferrous sheet metal. These are small, bench top presses and they are way too slow to work as a forging press, but some smiths are using air assisted hydraulic bottle jacks in a substantial frame with good success in forging. These are usually a less expensive alternative to the hydraulic forging press but may have limitations in speed, power and size for what you want to achieve as a forging press.

A bench top bottle jack press, hand operated by PotterUSA (© KPotter)

Some smiths are using **hydraulic log splitters** for their forging presses. In many cases they are operated horizontally which takes up more floor space and is an awkward way of forging. Many use the gasoline engine that came with it for power so using this in a closed shop is a problem for carbon monoxide poisoning. Also the structure is not sufficient enough for a forging press and can crack or break with this use. They are designed to split wood, pushing something that gives, therefore the frame isn't as strong as what is required for forging against a material that doesn't want to give. However, the modern log splitters can be found with electric motors and they even rotate to a vertical position. This would be a better option. There is information on using these log splitters with conversion details in a book that I will refer to later.

A **hydraulic forging press** uses hydraulics instead of inertia or a dropping hammer to produce its force. It can be used similar to the power hammer in regards to being used with open dies, (two flat plates), or with quick change tooling or dies. Instead of hitting the metal it uses its power to squish it like modeling clay. "Squish" is a technical term in a forging press.

Hydraulic forging presses are used for forging, upsetting, drawing out, fullering, punching holes, texturing, coining, hot and cold bending, straightening and more.

I would recommend looking up online videos of these machines in operation to learn more about which ones may be beneficial for the type of items that you want to produce. Contacting their builders can give you even more information on how they would work for your requirements.

I should also state that I am not saying that it is impossible for the other machines, especially the power hammer, to achieve what is done on the press, but in order to do so would take a much bigger machine which would also be more expensive than a hydraulic forging press and you still would not have the control that you get with the press.

The two machines that offer the most common functions in what they can do for the blacksmith shop are the power hammer and hydraulic forging press. I will give you some comparisons of those two machines. From now on I will use the term "press" meaning a "hydraulic forging press".

4 Comparing a Press to a Power Hammer

In operation there are differences between a press and a power hammer. A power hammer has an *intermittent* force. It hits, raises up and hits again repeatedly until the desired effect is achieved or heat is lost. A press has a *consistent* force. There is one squish until the desired effect is achieved or the metal is too cold to push any further. Both can *eventually* achieve the same end result.

Let us say that we are forging a steel bar that is 1-1/2" square. If the power hammer is too small for the work being done the sides of the hot bar will start to buckle under so that you have concave sides. The power hammer is pushing more material on the outside of the bar than from the inside. The same thing can happen on the end of a bar that is being hand hammered. That's why in drawing out a bar you end up with a pucker on the end. You needed a bigger hammer or stronger hammer blows with more heat. A bigger power hammer would produce sides that will be curved out or convex. You then had enough force to push the whole material at once.

A press will always produce convex sides or there will be too much material to push and the press will just stall, not pushing at all. This power pushing through the entire hot work is why a press does such a good job of forge welding and why knifemakers like them so much.

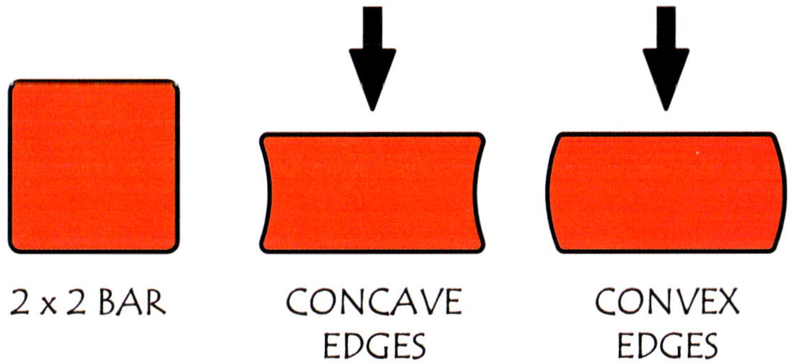

How hot metal moves under pressure. Too light a force will only move the outside of the bar. More than enough power will move the whole volume of the bar and the sides will bulge out.

This may be where the adage comes from that the power hammer works the metal from the outside of the bar and the press from the inside of the bar. That is not true if the power hammer is big enough. Then the press and the power hammer would be moving the metal the same way. The difference may come in regards to the size of hammer required to do the same job as a press of what ever tonnage and what size bar you are working.

Pros of the Press:

There is no foundation required for a press as in the older design power hammers. It does not have to be bolted down to the floor. You can even put casters on the base and move it where the press is needed or out of the way. This is because there is no shock or energy transferred to the base. All of the energy is between the ram and anvil plates.

A press has a small footprint compared to a power hammer of similar force, so not much floor space required.

There is no shock to the operator in operating a press as in hammering. This is beneficial to prevent future body ailments and for those with arthritis or other strength or joint problems.

The slower press operation allows you to align parts with each squish compared to the lightning fast operation of a power hammer.

In many designs of presses you operate a press standing up instead of leaning over compared to operating a power hammer. This is due to the anvil being closer to your eye height on the press.

In addition to sharing some common operations a press can do some unique forming operations that cannot be achieved with a power hammer.

It is easy to make a quick change die system for the press. The use of dies is a great way to form repeated shapes with ease.

A press can be used as a brake for bending, either with the metal hot or cold depending on the size of the material and amount of the bend.

Usually the press is a quieter machine as it does not have the constant banging sound of hammering, but it still has the whine of the motor and especially the pump running. There are companies that make a suppressor attachment for the hydraulic system. This is an in-line device that suppresses the hydraulic noise, shock, vibration and pulsation of your hydraulic system from the pump and the hoses. If you mount your tank, motor and pump on a cart you can put that unit in another room away from you and hear no noise from it. Earplugs also work wonders. There are also designs with a submergible pump that mounts *in* the hydraulic fluid tank. This also works to quiet the noise of the press.

In talking to others about their presses I ask, "what do you like about your press?" and the answer most often is, "control, control, control!"

A press is economical. Generally it is a lot less expensive to buy or build than a power hammer of comparable power.

Cons of the Press:

It does have safety issues that you do not have with a power hammer.

There is a danger of pieces flying out of the press and that danger is relative to the increasing tonnage of the press you are using. If you put a piece in the press wrong and it gets away from you it could throw it at you causing very serious injury to you.

There is the problem of hydraulic fluid being flammable in a forging shop. Hydraulic fluid can ignite at 438 degrees F, so a gas or coal fire could easily ignite this fluid.

A pin hole leak in the high pressure hoses at high pressure can cut off fingers or cause other damage and if ignited becomes a flame thrower that could burn you and burn down your shop. A smaller hole can spew out a mist that produces a cloud that can ignite and kill you as it sucks the oxygen out of your lungs or cause severe burns.

Hot metal used in the press has constant contact with the anvil and ram plates or tooling. This allows the heat in your hot work to be transferred into the plates or tooling which cools the hot work and heats up the plates/tooling. Your tooling is now very hot requiring tongs or clamping pliers to cool or to change your tooling. Smaller metal may not stay hot long enough to get the same amount work done as it would on a power hammer where the hot work would bounce on the tooling and not have a chance for the heat to transfer. Sheet metal does not have much resistance in forming and works very well in a press.

Heat can be lost in your work by the cold tooling/dies sucking the heat away from the metal, but in some circumstances the friction actually increases the heat of the work. In pressing thinner material, especially with bronze or tool steel, the heat can be drawn out of the work so fast that you can have work hardening and breakage of your work unless you pre-heat the dies. This could also become a safety issue with fragments being thrown at you.

In pattern welded steel work, forge scale can be pushed into the work which can ruin the surface of your work. Wire brushing the surface before pressing can help to resolve this issue. Flux can help prevent this, too.

Fortunately there are precautions which can be taken to prevent all of these things from happening. See the "safety" area below.

Things that are the same with both a power hammer and a forging press:

They both require a power source, usually 220 volt electric.

They both move/forge hot metal.

They both have safety issues and an understanding of forging will make utilizing these machines more beneficial to you.

They both require some maintenance. Both need to be inspected, oiled and/or greased for smoother operation.

5 Press Construction

Learn as much about forging presses as you can BEFORE you build or buy one. This way you will get one that will do what you require and that will last you safely for years.

Here is some information to help you decide what type of press you need:

What Makes Up A Press?

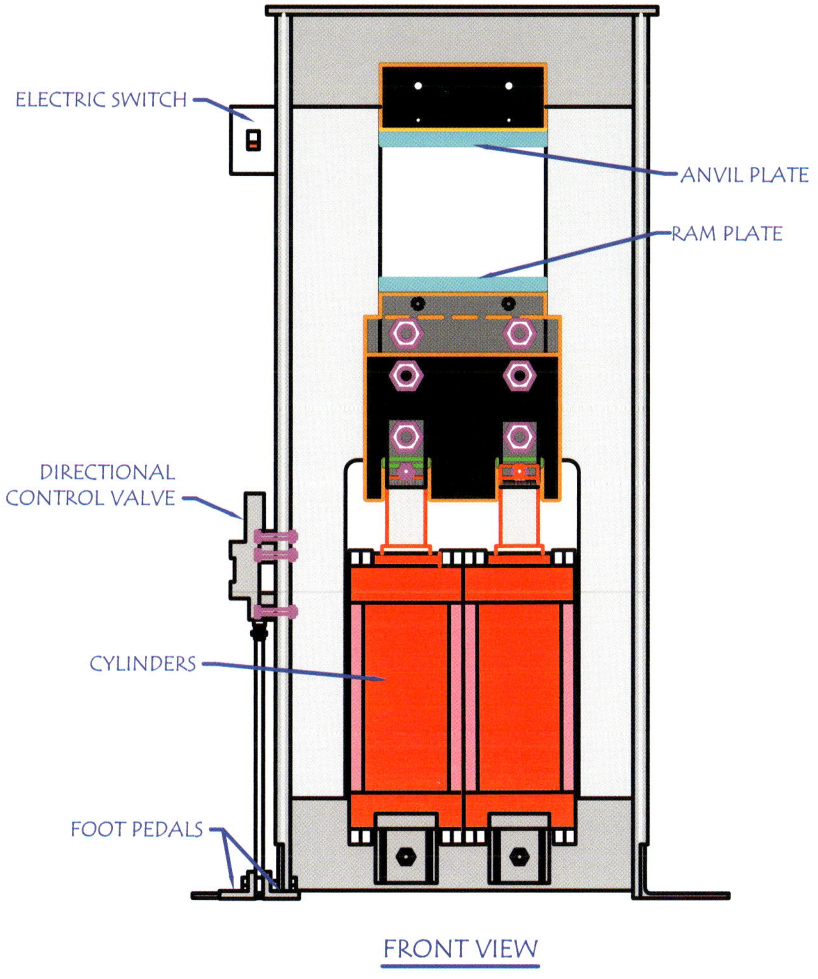

Basic parts to an H-frame press

In other words what are the parts to a press that all presses have in common? First they all have a structure or framework that supports the work load and power source. The form and structure of the frame depends on the materials used to build it, the tonnage that it must support and ease of use depending on what is being made with the press.

They have a hydraulic cylinder or cylinders. A hydraulic cylinder converts the energy of the hydraulic fluid into a safe, controlled force in a linear direction. For our purposes they are double acting hydraulic cylinders. This means there is power used for both extension and retraction of the cylinder rod.

To keep the power of this cylinder rod running in a straight and safe direction a ram slide or ram guide is required. This connects to the end of the cylinder rod and either wraps around a web on the press frame or is somehow held in place as it travels up and down its length in operation.

Anvil and ram plates, also known as platens, are what support your work or your work and tooling. The anvil plate is the non-moving plate and the ram plate is on the end structure of your cylinder rod that moves.

The mechanicals are what operate the cylinder. We are using a fluid power system and are using hydraulic oil to transfer the power. The two stage pump regulates the flow of oil in the hydraulic system and converts the mechanical power of the electric motor into hydraulic energy. It must create a high volume of flow and force to make the cylinder operate fast enough and with enough force to produce the tonnage required.

As you may have noted above, we also have an electric motor to power the pump. There are also low pressure and high pressure hoses, an oil filter and a storage tank for the hydraulic oil.

A hydraulic control valve, also called a directional control valve is used to control the flow of the hydraulic fluid to the cylinder. This controls the cylinder rod to operate up or down.

This is just a basic idea of what we are working with in a hydraulic forging press. Other parts will be covered later.

You can not just see a press that you think that you like and ask what size this or that is because you want to build one like that one. These have to be complete packages designed to work together. The frame, cylinder, pump and motor have to be right for each other or you may have a disastrous event.

Here is more information about differences in presses and figuring what is the best configuration for you.

What Tonnage Do You Need?

What are you planning on making with your press? How big are these pieces you want to make? What forging operations will you be doing to the material? Those are the biggest questions to ask yourself. Remember tonnage is rated per square inch so if doing a 3” wide piece with 3” square dies you’ve lost about 2/3’rds of your power. Press speed is also a factor.

Here are some examples of job size related to press size:

Pattern welded steel forging and knife blade work usually use narrow pieces of steel so 24 tons is a big enough press in most cases. It can still do a lot more than just that, too. This is because of the operations you are doing and the size of your work. In fullering you either have a top and bottom fuller or a top fuller and anvil plate. So the width of the tooling pushing on the work is also narrow.

Therefore it does not take any more force to move your hot material. Some knife makers want to be able to make bigger billets so they move to a 35 to 50 ton press. When I say bigger billets it is not the height of the stack of metals but the width that requires more tonnage. Instead of pushing a stack of metal that is 1” wide by ever how long, when it is pushing a stack that is 2-1/2” wide or more it requires more power due to the tonnage per square inch. Again with narrow tooling 24 tons may still be more than enough power.

Many architectural smiths are working in wider and thicker material and may be doing more die work such as forms and texturing. They use from a 45 ton to a 100 ton press. This is plenty for up to 2-1/2” square steel, but if they do larger forging than that they may go to a 150 to 200 ton press.

Some smiths that do a wider range of work have a couple different size presses. The bigger presses have more power but have lost some of the control of the smaller presses. The bigger press can just push right through the smaller material and make it too thin.

I use a 60 ton press and in most cases this is more than required. I have made top and bottom dies to create sea shells that are about 5” square. I use 3/16” thick mild steel sheet for the shells and the press grunts to get the job done. I usually have to heat the pieces three times or more in order to put the shape and especially the detail into these items. Their large size has significantly spread the contact surface and thus reduced the tonnage per square inch. For this job I wish I had at least a 100 ton press.

I have figured out a way I can get maximum use of the tonnage I do have in cases where I need more tonnage due to the material area requiring more power to get the job done. Instead of squishing the whole area of the material at once I use a top tool that is 1 inch square or round. That keeps the maximum tonnage of the machine, but then I have to move the top tool over a section at a time on the work to get the full press on the material. The problem can be with this is that you may not get the same depth of push in each area. In using a top and bottom die, as in the shell design, that is not a problem.

I hope I have not confused you. Again, the tonnage you choose is relative to what you are making, its size and what operations you are doing and always keeping in mind that it does not get so big that it obliterates your design or objective. I hope these examples help.

Ideally if you could try even one press and see how it works for what you want to do and the maximum size material you want to work with, then you would have some gauge as to whether you need a more or less powerful press than the one you sampled.

Speed in Press Operation

Speed is one of the most important factors in a press. It is what makes it a *forging* press. Your pump and matching motor will determine the speed and force of your system and so should be determined by the maker of the press or the chart that shows you what pump you need for your cylinders. You will not be running the full length of the cylinder rod, but just the opening with your work in it. Still in that distance you want the press to be fast yet have control of what you are doing.

I heard one of the best explanations of force and speed in a response to a question about the comparison of forces generated by a 20 ton hydraulic forging press made from a hydraulic cylinder versus a press made from a 20 ton air over hydraulic jack:

"That is a strange question as 20 tons is 20 tons, however if you are talking about forging it's not all about force generated. When you are forging a large part of how much work you can do is speed related. A fast 10 ton press will do far more work than a slow 40 ton press. Fast and powerful requires big pumps and complex hydraulics (dual pump setups with pressure bypasses) I have built 10 presses or so and with each one it seems like I try to step up the pump size and often put in a smaller cylinder. I think the ideal set up for forging would be a 20 GPM single stage pump and about a 6" cylinder. That would give you 35 tons and a extend speed of about 5 seconds per foot. A press set up like this would be fantastic for punching and general forging. It would also do more work than a 100 ton press that moved at 30 seconds per foot. The issue is that to get 20 GPM at 2600 PSI in a single stage pump it takes a 25-30 HP motor which makes it unreasonable for most shops. You can skirt this a bit by using a two stage pump such as the 10 HP 16/4 GPM unit ... It is not ideal as the speed slows down right when you need it but there simply is no other good option if you want high tonnage and speed.

The other thing is what you hope to do with the press. If you want to do embossing, bending or straightening speed is not as critical. If you want to make large sectional changes it (speed) is more important." –Larry Langdon

I was concerned with the type of work that I do in making dies that this would be just too fast to position my tooling and control of the depth of each push. I asked Larry at what point do you loose control with that speed and if that is a problem?

Larry responded: "It does become a problem. I have experimented with speeds that became problematic for positioning; however they worked fantastic for production work placed with jigs."

Larry's general forging press runs about 2 inches per second during the high speed pressure and a half inch per second during high pressure. After seeing his video of that press operating I do not think I would want one any faster than that for the type of work that I do. The faster speed would also require limit switches to control the depth of the push. More on limit controls later.

My press is also about 2.18 inches per second and I am very satisfied with that speed. It is good for general forging operations and for die work. The press book that I will refer to in Chapter 5 would be a good reference to have in purchasing a press as well as building a press. There are charts to figure ram speed based on the size of cylinders and the flow of the pump and other good information that would be of benefit in either circumstance.

Cycle Times

Cycle times in press use are not really a factor. There is no hesitation or waiting for something else to happen before it is ready to go again. You run the press to the desired depth, open it back up and then squish again. The only delay is in the time it takes to move your foot to hit the controls.

Press Structure/Framework

There are different designs for the press framework. Here are the designs, benefits and restrictions of the smaller presses made for blacksmiths and knife makers. Industrial presses small enough to be used in a blacksmith shop will also be covered:

C-Frame Press

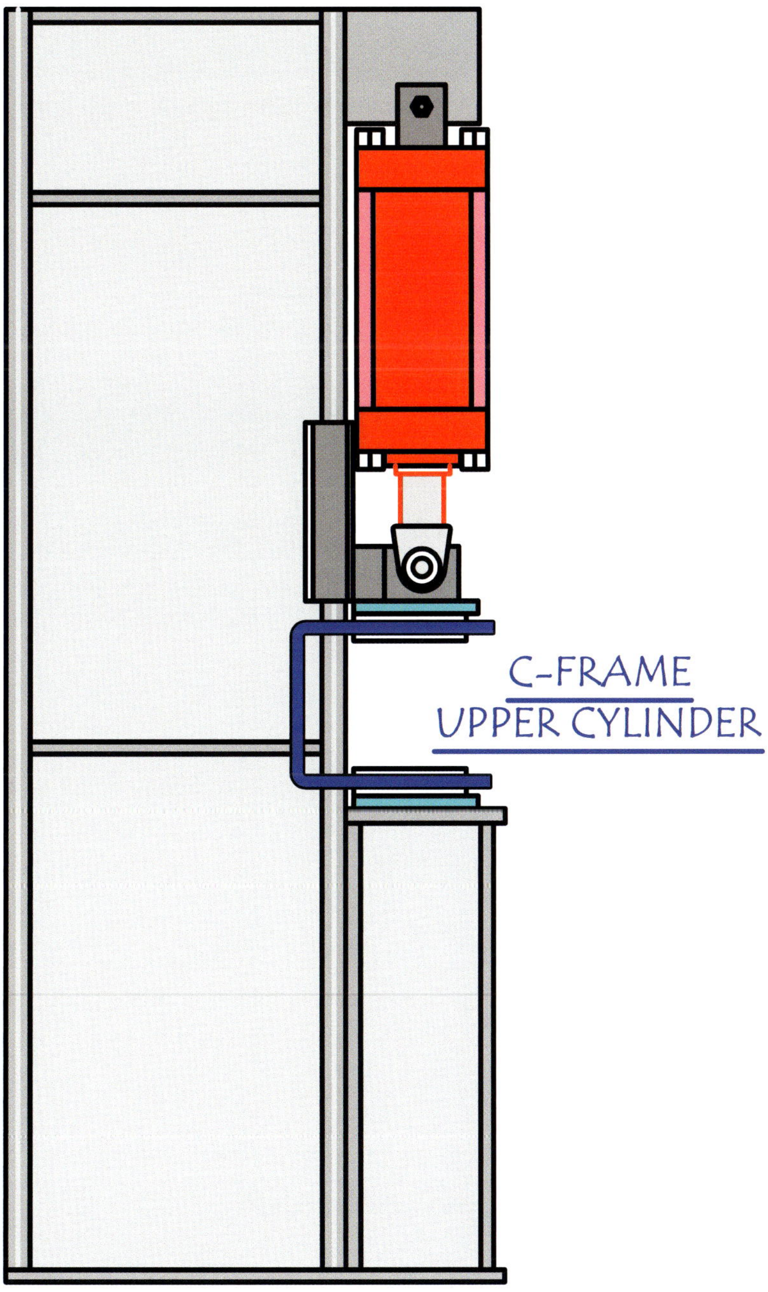

This usually has a vertical post of a heavy wall steel I-beam which may have steel plates welded to it for more strength. The ram and anvil are mounted to one flat side. The ram is mounted around one web of the I-beam for the ram travel guide. Since everything is mounted to one side the front of the anvil plate and ram plate are open to one side giving the appearance of a "C".

It may have a smaller footprint than an H-frame press.

This usually supports smaller tonnage due to construction strength factors.

Most blacksmith C-frames are 30 tons and below. One reason for the lower tonnage is that the ram/anvil plates are only supported from one side, the side that runs along the I-beam. Higher tonnage than this can flex the I-beam unless that is figured into its construction.

Having one open side to access your tooling/dies with your hot metal is easier as you are not trying to aim for a rectangular hole to put your metal in. The only restriction to your dies is the distance from the center of the dies to your post. This is usually closer than in an H-frame design and therefore your tooling is not as wide as on an H-frame press.

The height of the anvil plate can be low as in a power hammer or high for standing straight up while using it.

H-Frame Press

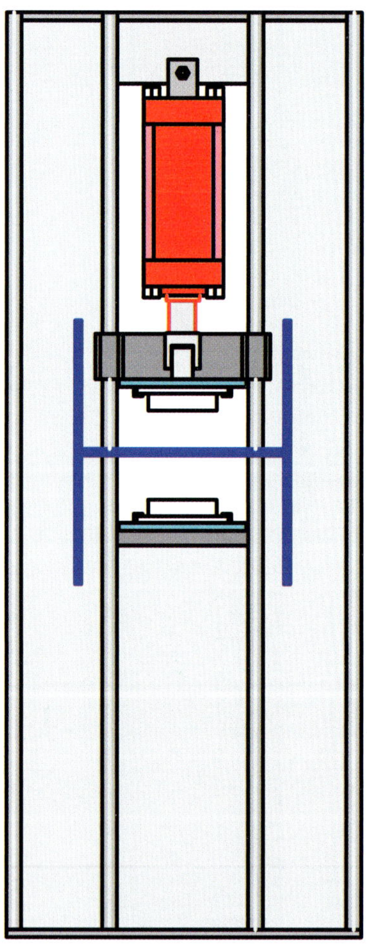

H-FRAME
UPPER CYLINDER

The H-frame press has a post on either side of the anvil and ram. This can either be from two separate I-beams or one large I-beam with the center cut out to receive the cylinder, ram and anvil. I have also seen these made using large heavy wall square tubing.

The ram plate runs in guides from both sides. The two posts with the horizontal plates between them are why it has the designation of an H-frame press.

This design is better for higher tonnage presses. There is less chance of twisting or bending of the frame, therefore less chance of breaking or cracking the welds during use. Having the ram guides supported from both sides also adds a lot of strength to this design.

This configuration provides a safer frame for high tonnage presses. It has an enclosed opening. It could be a problem if you are doing work that is larger than the opening or something like a large bowl that you are working from the center towards the edge.

The anvil plate on H-frame presses is usually high so you can see to aim at the opening and you stand up in use.

My opening is 7" high and 11" wide. I would not want it any smaller than this and would prefer a higher opening. Tooling can take up a lot of opening space and then it becomes restrictive to putting your metal between your tooling. I thought that an adjustable anvil plate configuration would be beneficial. If there were several large bolt holes in the frame that would allow the anvil plate assembly to be moved it could be closed down for smaller work with no tooling and opened up when using tooling and also for taller pieces of hot metal. Of course in planning this it must be done without compromising the strength of the frame. The bolts would also have to support the tonnage of the unit. The taller a piece of work the better chance there is of this flying out at you. Some type of holding or fixture devise may be required in this case.

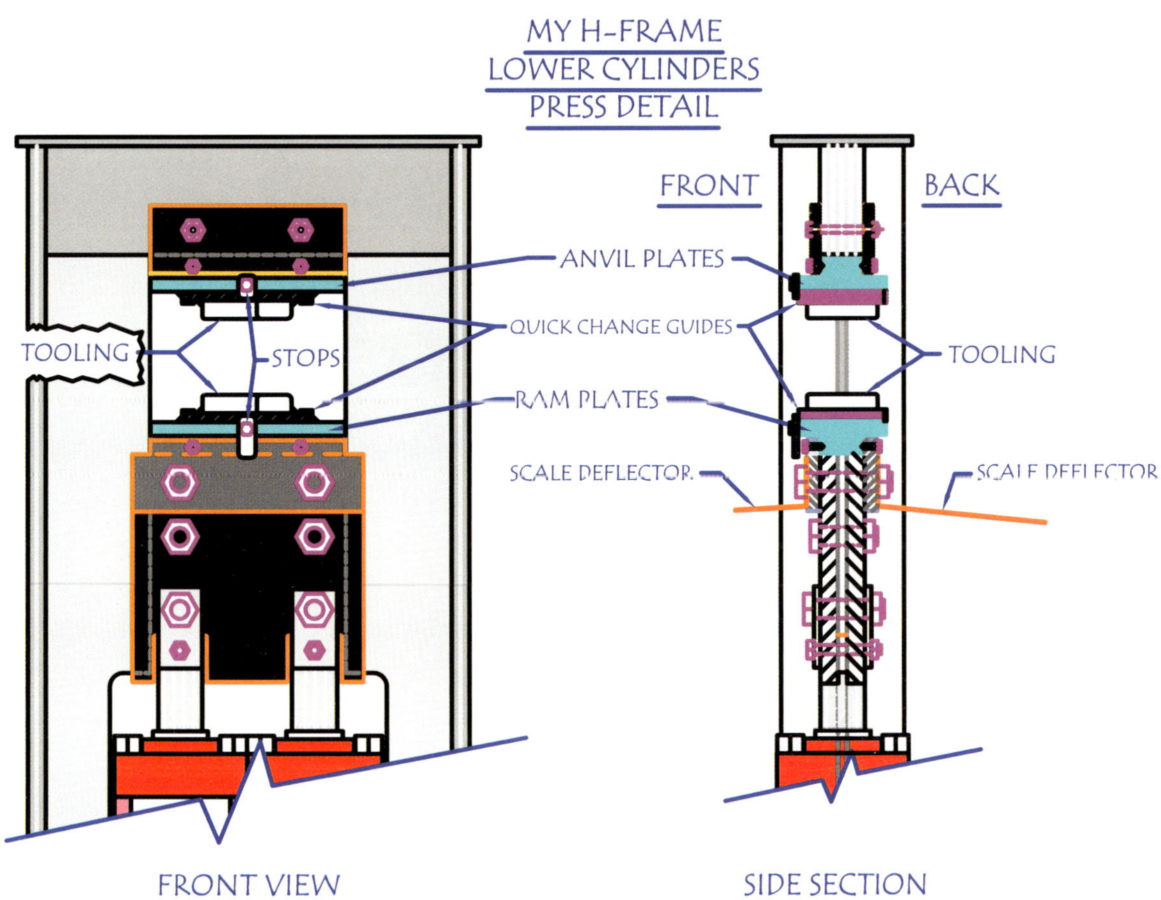

Parts of a hydraulic forging press

Two and Four Post Press

Matt Harris' four post, 200 ton forging press

These are usually industrial presses made by and for industrial shops. They are either one post on either side the ram and anvil plates, therefore a two post press, or they have four round posts on the corners that the ram plate slides over making it a four post press. They are made using specific heavy duty castings instead of I-beams and are usually made for higher tonnage presses, but I have seen them in as low as a 50 ton press for industry.

I should add that industrial presses have provided a solution for smiths looking for a press and are reluctant to build one or wait for one to be built. Some times they are also less expensive. Keep in mind that all hydraulic presses are not forging presses. Some were made to run slower for other operations instead of forging as in punching or working cold metal. Obtain as much information about how a specific press was used to get some idea if it will work for you or not. There are on-line used equipment companies that deal in these machines.

I have seen industrial presses in two posts, four posts, C-frames and H-frames. The C-frames and H-frames are much different looking than the I-beam presses, but still have that shape to them. Due to their construction they usually have more tonnage than our I-beam presses.

Many of these will already have limit switches included to control the height and depth of each push. This can be very advantageous.

Horizontal Presses

Horizontal presses are also found in industrial presses. The cylinder and ram run horizontally instead of vertical. These are usually known as upsetting presses as that is their main function. They even use hydraulics for clamping the work in place when upsetting. Limit switches are used to control the length of the push for upsetting so that every piece is exactly the same. This can be used for upsetting on the end of the bar or due to its' clamping feature any where down the length of the bar. As in other industrial presses these are found in a variety of sizes. One shop I was in had a row of upsetting presses and each one was about four feet wide, five feet high and twelve to fifteen feet long. I have seen others that were half of that size.

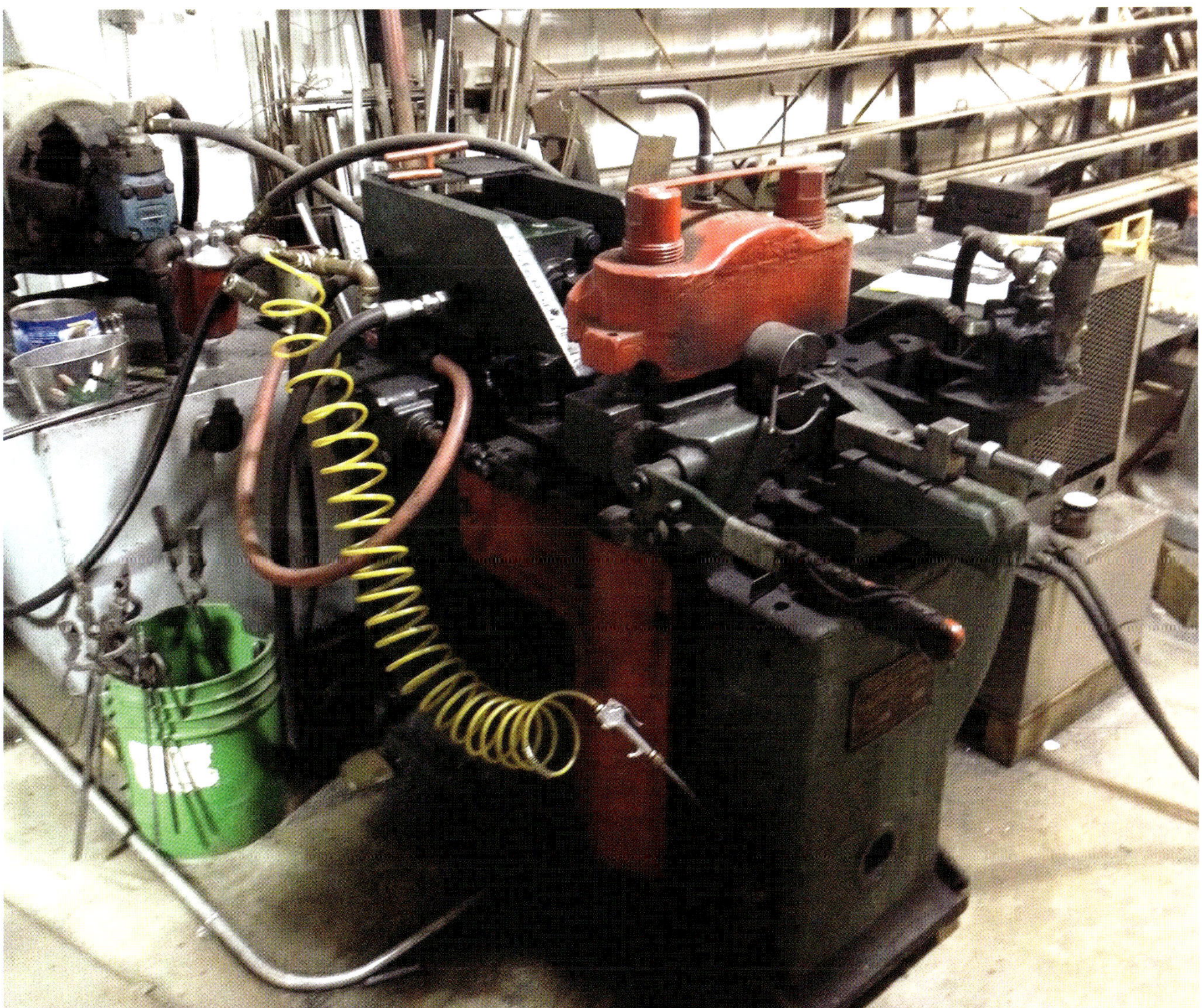

An industrial horizontal upsetting press (© DKayne)

In the gallery you will see photos of a homemade horizontal press used as an upsetting press and for other operations that can be raised to vertical when required. It also uses hydraulic clamps and limit switches. This takes a good machinist with a lot of knowledge of hydraulics and engineering.

I would recommend you learn as much as you can about any press you are interested in purchasing and thoroughly go over it to make sure all the frame and construction, valves, fittings and hoses are in safe working order. Replace anything that seems dubious and add any safety items that will be discussed later. Replacing the hydraulic oil and oil filter would also be recommended. Some industrial presses only have flat anvil and ram plates with a couple of tapped holes for attaching tooling or fixtures as they use them for the same operation repeatedly. If you plan on using quick change tooling note what arrangements would have to be made to make that possible. Some industrial presses have keyways or other systems which work well with quick change tooling and fixtures.

Cylinder Location

The cylinders for a press are double acting hydraulic cylinders, meaning that they operate in both directions, pushing and pulling.

A cylinder ***above*** the working area requires more head room for the machine and pushes down. This upper cylinder arrangement can be top heavy and depending on the design may need to be mounted solid to the floor, though I have seen many with a wider base with the mechanicals underneath and casters being utilized. This puts the ram plate on top and the anvil plate on the bottom similar to a power hammer.

This system can put hoses, cylinder, pump and motor at your head level and can be more dangerous in a mechanical failure. Some designs of overhead cylinders have a safety shield around the cylinder in case of an emergency.

A cylinder ***below*** the working area provides a more compact and shorter unit and therefore can weigh less than the cylinder above design, but it usually pushes up instead of down. The lower cylinder arrangement puts the anvil plate on top and the ram plate on the bottom. You get used to working this way after one or two squishes so it is not a problem.

All of the operating mechanism is lower and safer for use if problems arise.

Due to a lower center of gravity it can be used with casters for moving around. This is often a design for an H-frame press. I don't recall ever seeing a C-frame press with a lower cylinder not that someone hasn't done that.

I did see one industrial seventy ton two post press that had a lower cylinder, but the cylinder was placed upside down from usual. It was under the anvil plate and pushed down onto a movable cast steel plate where the posts were attached. The posts slide through bushings in a heavy cast anvil plate. So this put the ram plate on top and this press pushes down instead of up. Also as in many two or four post presses, the upper end of the posts are threaded so that you can raise or lower the top plate which changes the opening between your anvil and ram plates depending on the size of material you are squishing. This is a nice solution for those who do not like the pushing up scenario.

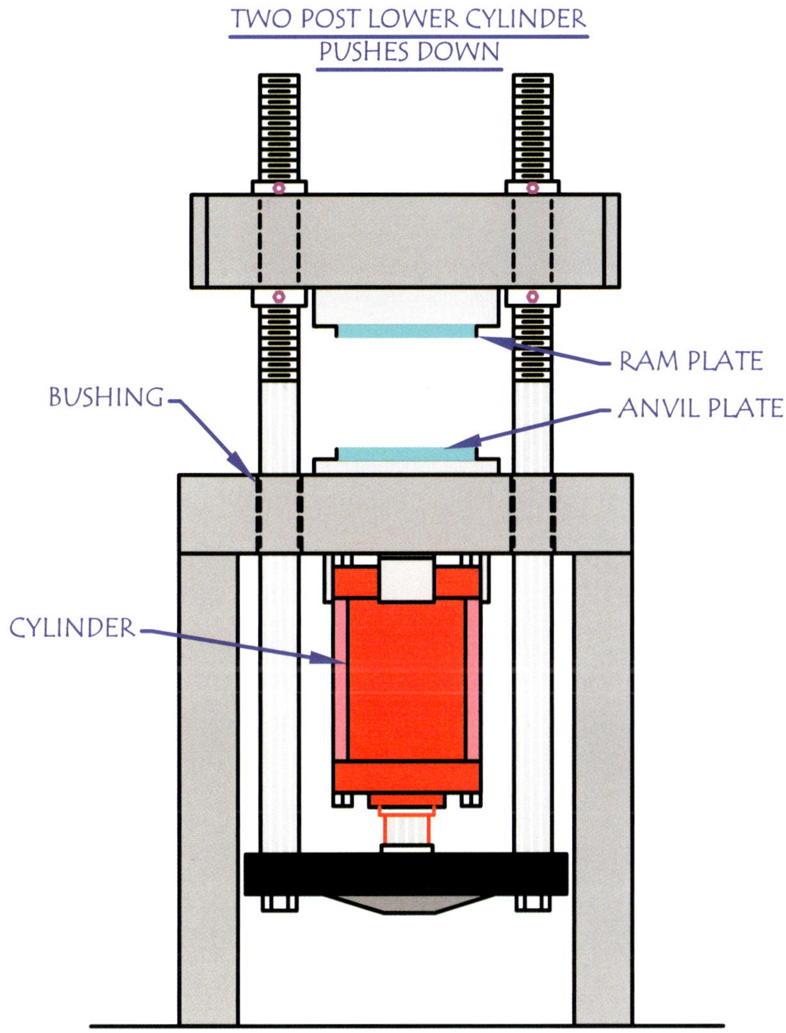

An unusual two post press with lower cylinder that pushes down

Recently I have found a blacksmith forging press with the lower cylinder pushing down and also plans to build such a press. More information on those presses later.

Single or Double Cylinders

The majority of presses have a single cylinder. In most cases that is all that is required. Even for higher tonnage presses one cylinder is enough, but in order to get that tonnage you need a bigger cylinder and bigger cylinders can be a lot more expensive. Some times you can get two smaller cylinders for less than one larger one. As an example my press has two six inch cylinders with 2-1/2" rods. A six inch cylinder is usually rated at about thirty tons at 2,240 psi, so two six inch cylinders in tandem at the same psi would be a sixty ton press. To do this in a single cylinder design would require a 12 inch cylinder which could cost three times the price of the two six inch cylinders.

I have been asked many times about how I synchronize the two cylinders so they both rise at exactly the same time. Actually that was one of my concerns when I bought it. The explanation is that pressure equalizes as long as the two cylinders are hooked up in tandem, then the oil will flow equally to both cylinders at the same time. This has not been a problem for me at all. I have seen that they do sell a synchronizer for this purpose.

Ram Guides

There are different ram guides for different configuration of press construction. The guide or guides are required to keep the ram running straight and fairly tight to your structure. Any play in this configuration will push your work in dangerous ways and will cause wear in your press. You will not have much say on which type of guide will be used as the type of guides depends on what you have to attach the guides to on your press.

Many C-frame presses have an I-beam for the support post and the flat side of the beam is where the cylinder gets mounted. Due to this the ram guide has a flat plate that lies on that flat side of the beam. This can either have plates that wrap around its flange on both sides or if there is a large enough surface a guide system mounted to the I-beam surface to keep the operation straight and true as the cylinder ram runs up and down the beam.

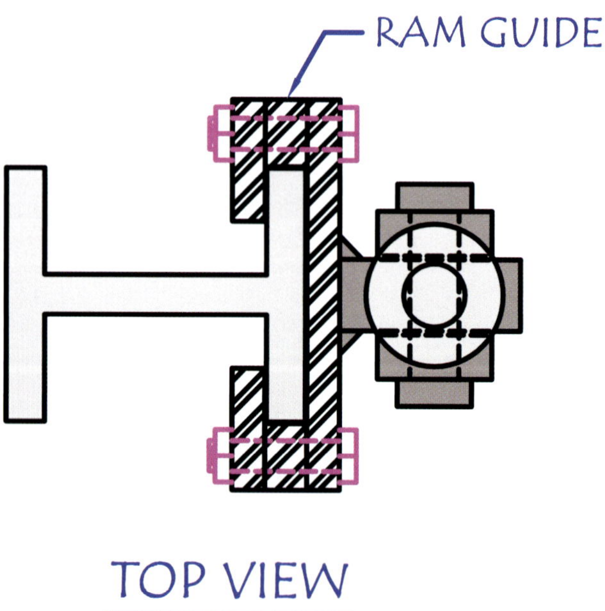

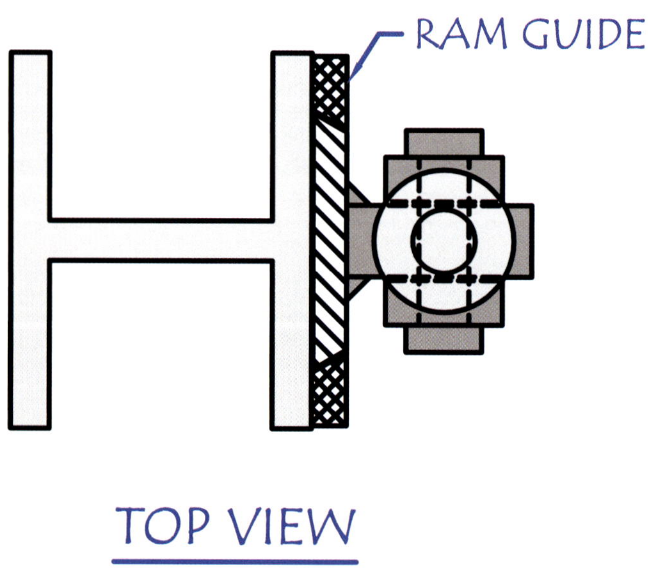

Two C-Frame ram guide configurations

The same type of guide is used on an H-frame press if the frame is made up of two separate I-beams with the cylinder in between them.

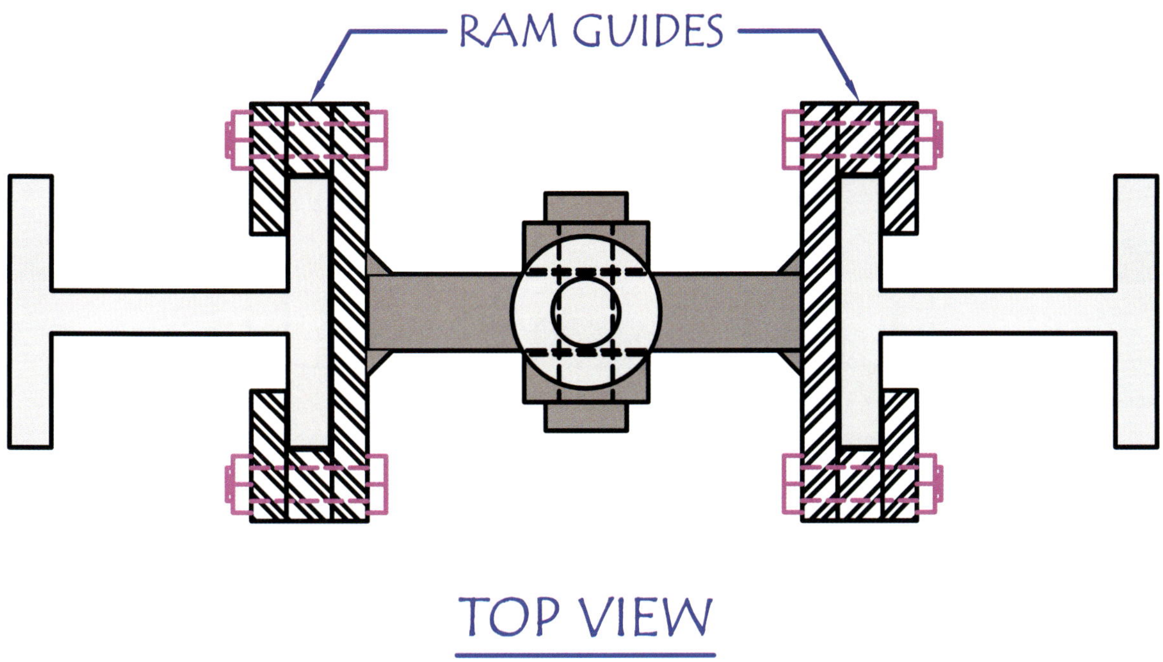

H-Frame with two I-beams ram guide configuration

Some H-frames are made from one large I-beam with the center web cut out to allow a place for the cylinder and ram and anvil plates. In this set up it is easy to have a guide made up of three plates. One plate that fits in the opening and two larger plates on either side of it that extend over the sides of the opening forming the travel guides on both sides.

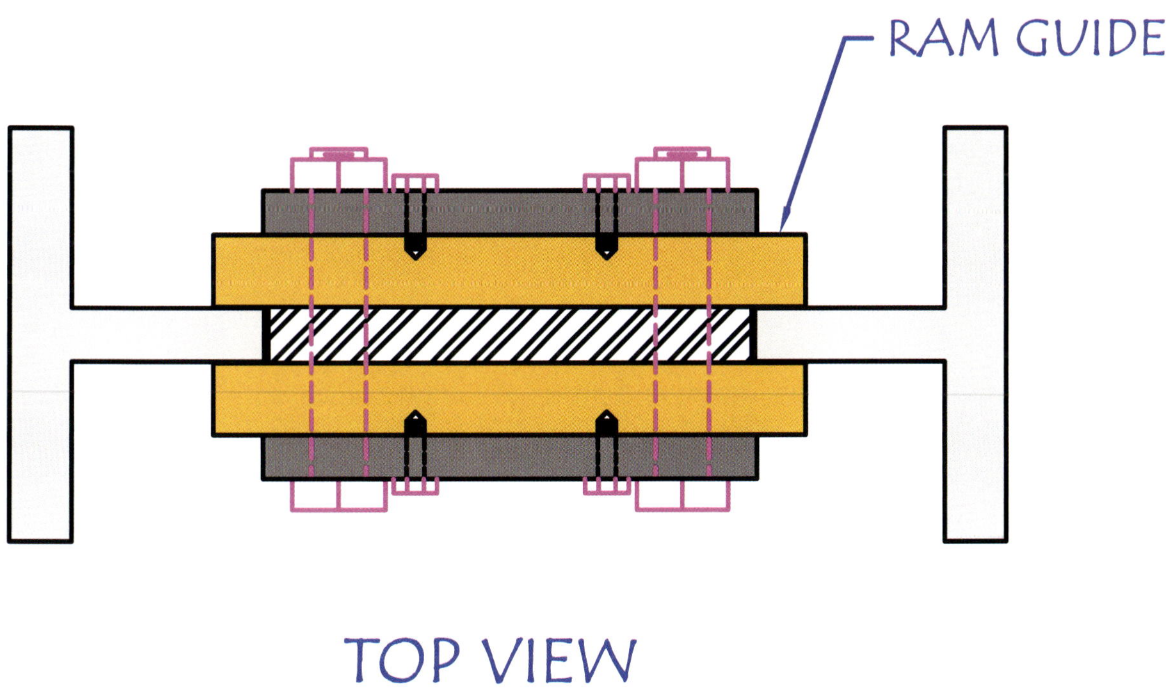

H-Frame I-beam with web cut in center, ram guide configuration

If the press is made from tubing instead of I-beams a single or double bar is welded for guides on the ram to run in or over depending on which configuration is used.

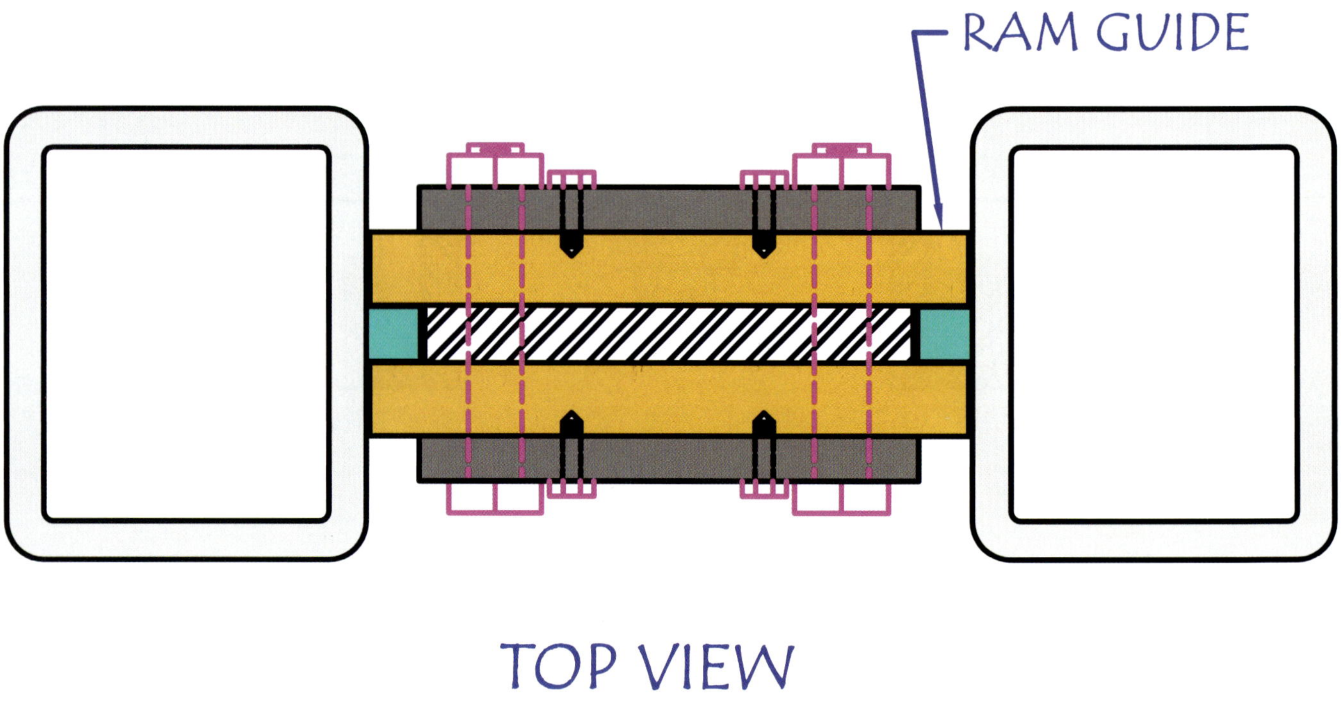

H-Frame from tubing ram guide configuration

Post style industrial forging presses use large bushings for their guides. These are usually in a hole in a steel casting to give them support.

Mechanicals Location

Attaching the hydraulic fluid tank, motor and pump to the press makes for a tidier, more compact unit. It also keeps hoses off of the floor. This also puts the noise and chance of mechanical failure closer to you. It also puts more vibration into the frame which could in time lead to weld failure. If you do use this system get as much of the mechanicals on the back of the unit as possible. Especially attach the hoses on the back of the press and have them protected from hot scale or hot metal. In instances where heavy wall tubing is used for the frame of the press I have also seen that tubing used for the hydraulic fluid storage tank.

If you do this, make sure you have some means for draining this tank; such as addind a treaded plug as low as possible.

Putting the hydraulic fluid tank, motor and pump on a cart can keep mechanical failures away from you. Putting this cart in another room will remove the noise of the motor and pump that is produced in operation. This does add concern about the safety of the hoses that run from the cart to the press.

The mechanicals cart for Randy's press

Directional Control Valve Activation

The directional control valve for Randy's press

Many of these handmade presses simply use the handle that comes along with the control valve as a means to raise and lower the ram. The valve is placed higher on the press and one hand is used to lower and raise the ram. The draw back to this is that you now only have one hand to control and move your hot metal in the press and no hand to use for handled top tools or for turning the press off or on. This also places the valve and hoses at head level which could be dangerous in case of equipment or hose failure.

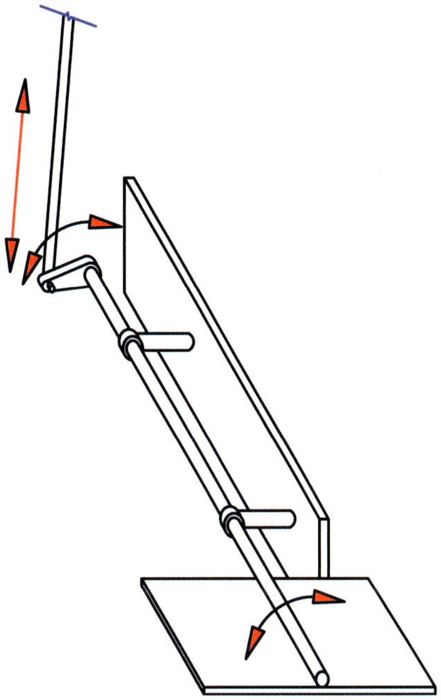

A hinged style foot pedal to raise and lower the control valve bar

It is simple to make a mechanical foot pedal system for your press. It can be a fixed rod that the pedal is mounted to on one end and hinges in the center so that it rotates from side to side. Step on one side and it pushes the valve up to close the ram, step on the other side and the rod goes down to open the ram. Another way is to have two separate pedals. One hinged on the far end with the control valve attaching rod in the center to pull the control valve down, the other pedal hinged in the middle to push the rod up when you push down.

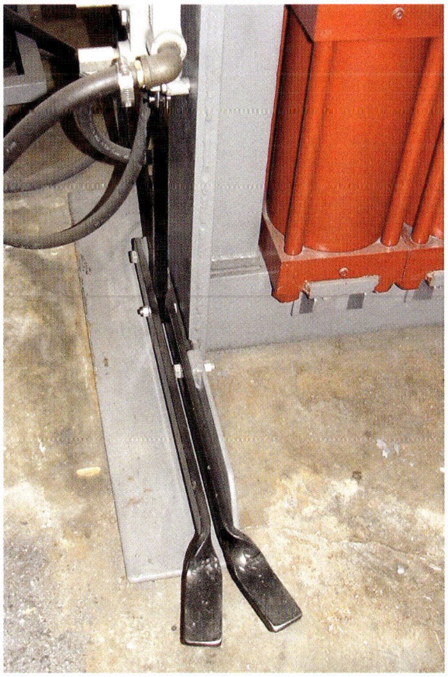

Front view of the pedal configuration on Randy's press

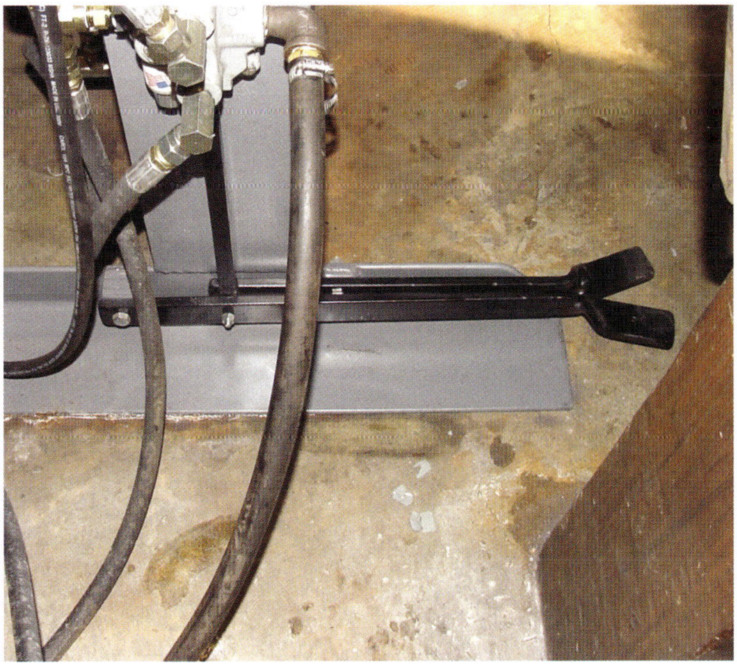

Side view showing the foot pedal hinge pin location on Randy's press

Another solution is to use an electric solenoid valve with an electric pedal. A hydraulic directional solenoid control valve operates when electric current is supplied to the solenoid instead of the mechanical movement of a manual valve. When you apply current to one side of the valve the press closes and when you apply it to the other side of the valve the press opens. One of the advantages of the solenoid system is that you can move the pedal where ever it is the most convenient to work as it is not attached by mechanical means but by an electric wire. Be sure this type of pedal has a cover that your foot goes into so that a piece of metal dropped can not operate the press in either direction by mistake and that the wire is protected from being crushed by heavy metal dropping on it or from burning.

Limit Switch

The configuration with an electric solenoid valve also makes it simple to add a limit switch system to your press. A limit switch adjusts how far the ram pushes up and down on each push and can be very advantageous in die work and other repeated operations. The limit switch is a simple on/off switch that can be attached to your press that connects to the solenoid. One or two limit switches can be slid over a threaded rod mounted on the front of your press. One switch if you only want to stop how deep the ram pushes, two switches if you want to stop how far the ram pushes and how far it opens before stopping and returning to push again. The switches are adjusted in height by locking corresponding threaded nuts on the top and bottom of each switch at the desired location on the threaded rod or locking a thumb screw if using a slide rod. When the ram plate comes past a switch it pushes against it and turns the solenoid on or off depending on how you have it set up. This system works great if you want the exact same item every time and saves you time, too, as it shortens the time running between pushing and opening of the ram plate/tooling.

Limit switch components (© FabLimited)

Mechanical pedals do not have a limit switch system but will often use stop blocks between the ram and anvil plates to stop the ram from pushing past a certain point. One problem with this, though it does work to some degree, is that you have to have many stop blocks depending on how far down you want the ram to stop. It will require room on your ram and anvil plates to place the blocks. It also does not stop as accurately as a limit switch and may damage your plates.

Quick change die systems

It is very advantageous to be able to quickly change your tooling and dies when operating your press. There are several simple ways to do this depending on the design of your press. Basically it is just a retaining block or heavy angle iron that allows a piece of steel with the tooling welded to it to slide in and out of the press. It holds the tooling plate in place while pushing or pulling the tooling while forging. Having these on the top and bottom ram/anvil plates automatically positions them for precise alignment.

C-frame presses have an open side from the ram and anvil plates so this makes it easy to slide tooling into guides that face to that open side. All of your tooling is installed from the side of the press, usually not the side you are working from. Still there are different configurations of guides to hold your tooling. I have seen some presses that use a rectangular block of steel with a groove cut on either long side to hold the tooling. The tooling would then be made like a side ways "C" shape with the ends of the "C" sliding into those grooves. It would take a flat plate that would lay on the press plate, two vertical side plates and two small horizontal plates to slide into the grooves.

C-FRAME QUICK CHANGE TOOLING SET-UPS

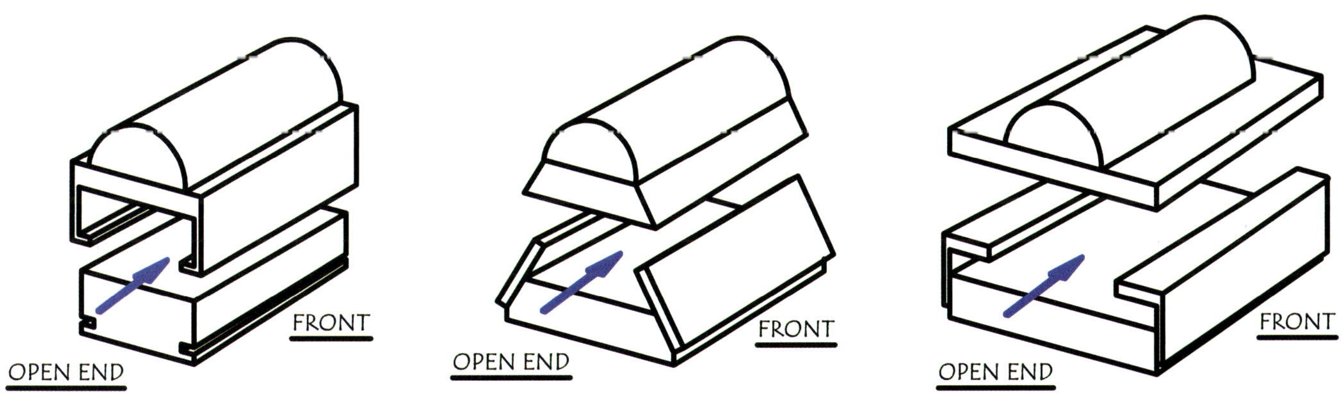

I have also seen the retaining guides attached to the angled sides that were machined into the plates creating a dovetail that the tooling plates slide into. The tooling plates would then have to have angled sides to fit that configuration.

Another solution is to use heavy wall angle iron or machine or fabricate two heavy duty "L" shape pieces to hold your plates and weld these to either side of your ram and anvil plates. These work as well as the other systems with the advantage of not having to machine or weld up your tooling plates each time you need a new tool. Tooling is easier and faster to make as it is just a flat plate.

The only draw back with this design in a C-frame press is that they take up more room on your plates than the other systems. If you know you will be working this way design wider plates in your press design and it will not be a problem.

A handle attached to the end of your tooling will make C-frame tooling easy to install and remove without the use of tongs or other tools. This handle can also be used as a hook for hanging your tooling on a tool rack, but put the tool surface facing out so that you can see which tool you want.

H-FRAME QUICK CHANGE TOOLING SET-UP

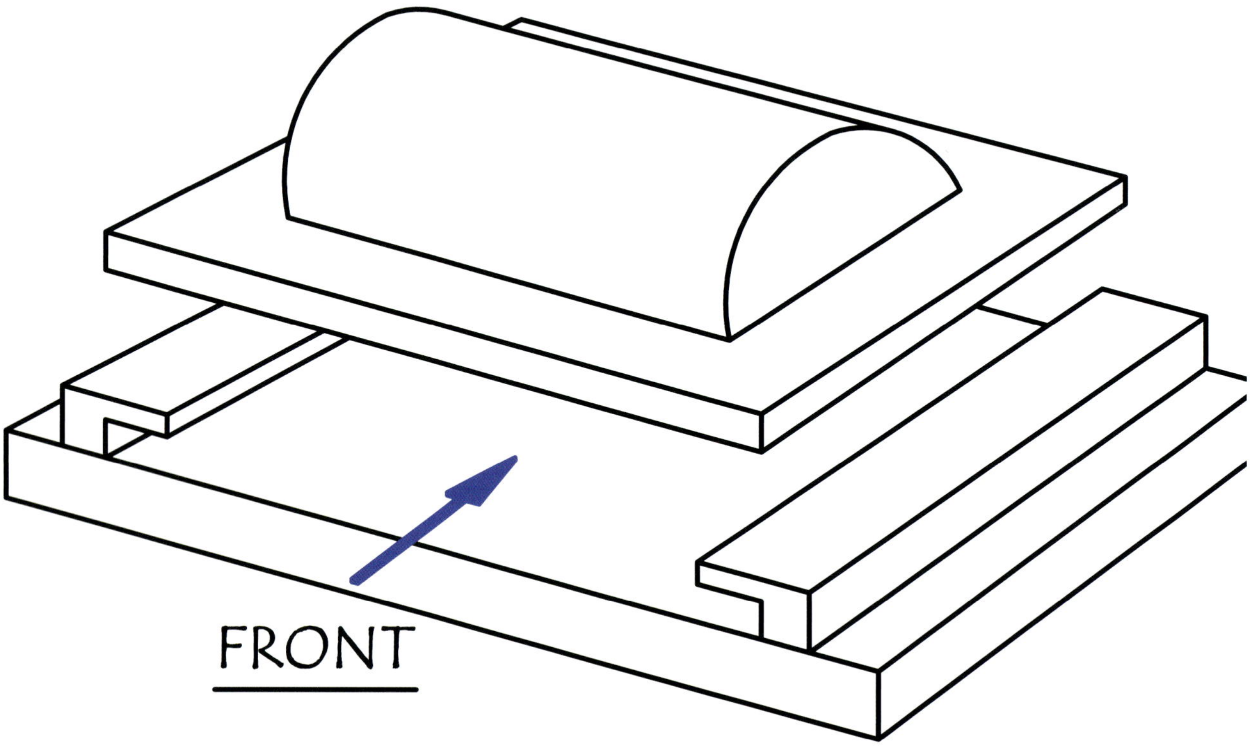

The H-frame presses use these same designs for their quick change tooling, but the tooling has to be loaded from the front instead of from the side. Be sure that you have a back stop and a front stop so that the tooling plate can not be thrown out of the guides and especially not towards you. This front stop is simply a piece of flat stock with a hole drilled off center and a bolt into a tapped hole in the ram and anvil plates so that any time you let go of it the stop automatically falls vertically blocking the tooling plate from coming out. It is similar to a shutter dog in operation. A simple ninety degree turn of the stop allows the tooling to slide past the stop.

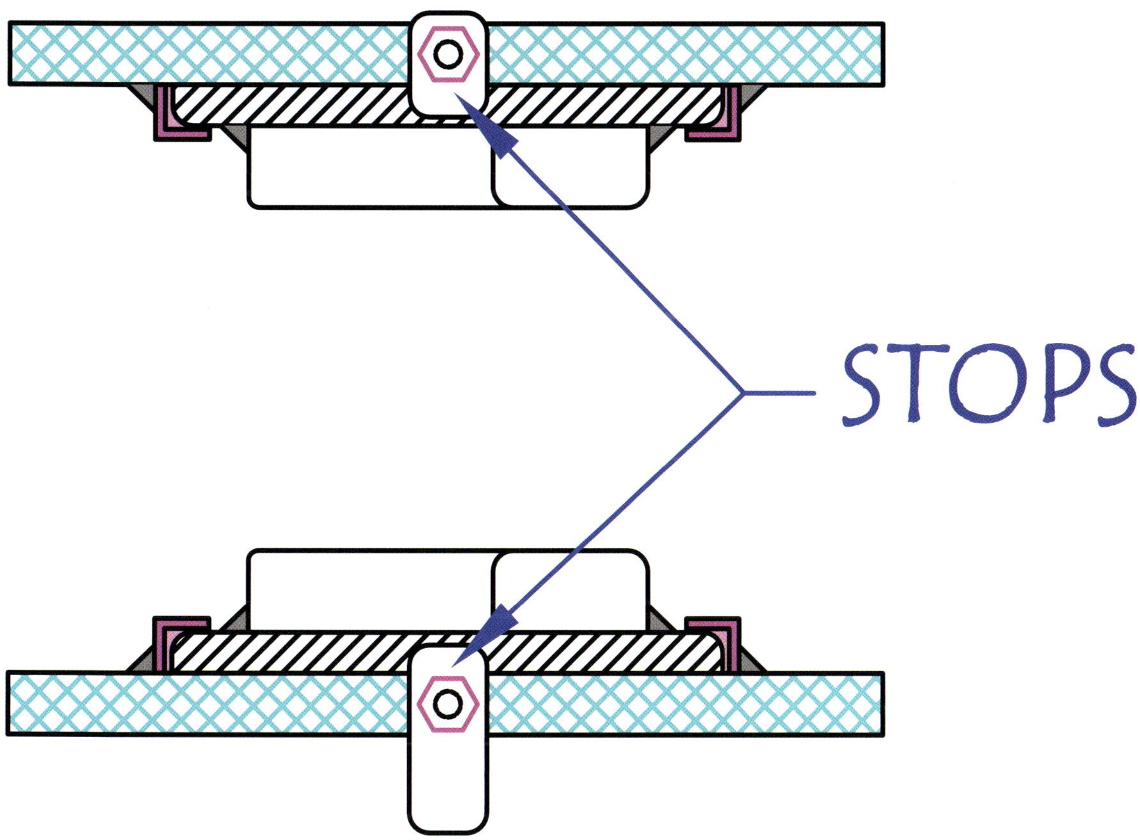

Top and bottom stops for quick change tooling plates

I make my tooling plates for my H-frame press an inch smaller than the depth of the ram/anvil plates. I place a half inch square bar on the back and the front of the tooling plate to center it on the plate. This way if something is out of alignment I can shim the plate with different bars to move the plate where needed.

I will share more information on tooling below.

One of the best things that I can suggest in press design and operation is to keep it simple. The more complex an arrangement you make the more you will have to do in repairs or in making tooling. These blacksmith/knifemaker presses work so why go nuts with adding this and that to complicate it and have more to go wrong. Find what works for you and go from there.

6 Build or Buy

Now, in considering this information, do I want to build my own press, have it built, or purchase one already made?

If you have the skills and knowledge to do this yourself I would recommend you get the book "Build Your Own Hydraulic Forging Press", by James L. Batson. This is the bible on homemade press construction. It includes plans for building a C-frame and an H-frame press and even a log splitter conversion. It has charts to figure out what cylinders and what mechanicals are required for what tonnage and information on structural loads so you build the proper frame structure for the power that you require. It can be purchased through the American Bladesmith Society website www.americanbladesmith.com.

There are also plans and a dvd for building a 24 ton lower cylinder that pushes down. This is currently available for $25.00 from Cliff Ohlenburger, 2029 County Rd. 110, Jack, AL 36346, firebirdforge@centurytel.net.

Here are some ready to go presses that were available at the time of this writing. Things change so contact information and production may or may not still be active and designs and prices may be different. This will get you started as to what is out there. These are not recommendations, just sources, in no particular order:

Carolina Custom Knives has two H-frame presses with lower cylinders. One is a single cylinder at 24 tons for $3,400 and a double cylinder at 50 tons for $5,600. Contact Tommy McNabb in Bethania, NC at (336) 924-6053. www.carolinaknives.com/press.html.

Ron Claiborne has an H-frame 25 ton press. He offers them as a cylinder above or a cylinder below design with a nice, compact design for the cart. They are currently sold through High Temperature Tools & Refractory for $5,000 and they have a one year waiting list for delivery. Contact Ron in Knoxville, TN at (865) 660-1569. www.hightemptools.com/hydraulicpress.html.

Carolina Custom Knives single cylinder, 24 ton press (©TMcNabb)

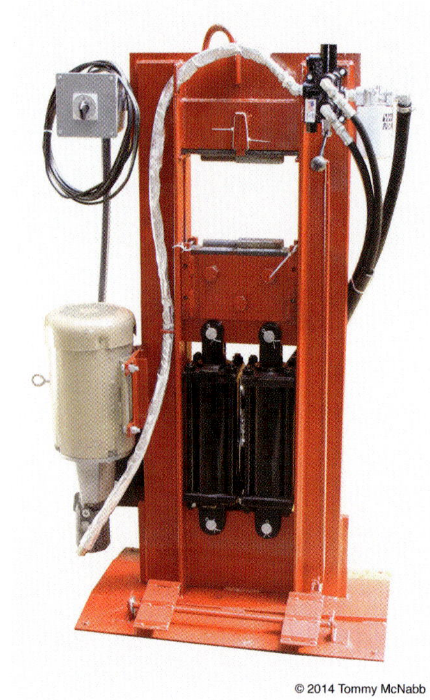

Carolina Custom Knives double cylinder, 50 ton press (©TMcNabb)

Claiborne 25 ton press

Claiborne press mechanicals cart

Riverside Machine sells Uncle Al's H-frame, 24 ton press. This is a lower cylinder that pushes down as I talked about earlier. It currently sells for $3,000, contact Al Lawrence at (870) 642-7643. http://w.ivenue.com/riversidemachine/ecommerce/uncleal-s-hydraulic-press.html

Uncle Al's 24 ton press, lower cylinder ram plate on bottom (©ALawrence)

The Jeff Carlisle, Imagination Xpress is a C-frame press, top cylinder, 15 ton press. Contact Jeff in Great Falls, MT at swain@3rivers.net for availability and pricing.

Jeff Carlisle, Imagination Xpress, 15 ton press (© JCarlisle)

Kevin Potter at PotterUSA, is making a forging press by taking his heavy duty bottle jack framework and has outfitted it with a hydraulic cylinder and mechanicals. The framework and casters under it raises it up so it sits on the floor and you stand at it in operation. One of the nice things about his system is that he is using a submergible pump in his hydraulic oil tank. This has quieted the noise of the pump down significantly. This 20 ton unit is currently $6,000. Website: www.potterusa.com, Phone: (520) 405-8539, email: sales@potterusa.com.

Potter USA hydraulic forging press, 20 tons (©KPotter)

There may be others producing presses, but these currently are the only ones advertising as such. You can do an internet search and see if you find others. Add "blacksmith" or "knife" or "damascus" to the word "press" and that will help to keep you away from the huge industrial presses. You may also look for used industrial hydraulic forging presses from equipment dealers. These could come out of industrial jewelry shops, foundries and other industry.

Asking about presses on web forums such as iforgeiron.com, metalartistforum.com, americanbladesmith.com, knifeforums.com and forums.dfoggknives.com may supply good leads for you, too.

Please compare what comes with each model and get the latest pricing and information on shipping or pick up. Some presses come with tooling of your choice and others do not. Many builders will custom build what you want in your press so if there is something you don't like in a particular model ask if you can buy it with what ever bells and whistles that you want.

Also realize you may have a waiting list to deal with, so plan accordingly.

7 Safety

As stated earlier the press can be a very dangerous machine, but if the following information is adhered to you will have a better chance of years of operation without any disastrous safety issues.

Press Safety

Do not skimp on materials or welding/bracing of the frame. Over build your frame. Better to have more strength than needed than not enough strength. You don't want it warping and twisting and popping welds and throwing pieces at you.

Use high strength bolts in the construction of your press. Inspect mounting bolts for wear or cracks. Replace when needed.

Make sure all fittings and hoses are top of the line hydraulic fittings.

Pay attention to the ram and anvil plates and quick change die system and the frame of your press under pressure, for twisting, bending and flexing or weld failure. Set a movie camera on a tripod and film a video of your press under operation to check these concerns as it is hard to see when you are running the press yourself. If there are any problems find a solution and fix it before any further operation of the press.

Inspect all tooling and dies for wear and cracks. Repair or replace when needed.

Inspect all hoses and fittings before each start. Look for wear or any leaks and repair them before operation.

This bares repeating: A pin hole leak at high pressure can cut off fingers or cause other personal injury and if ignited becomes a flame thrower that could burn you and burn down your shop. A smaller hole can spew out a mist that produces a cloud that can ignite and kill you as it sucks the oxygen out of your lungs or cause severe burns. The chance of this happening can be lessened by using protective sleeves on all high pressure hoses.

Hose sleeves on the high pressure hoses on the back of Randy's press.
Notice the zip ties holding the sleeves in place.

You have to disconnect one end of your hose from the fitting, slide the sleeve over it and reconnect the hose to the fitting. Slip ties work well for holding the sleeves in place. Currently they run around $4.00 per foot so will only cost you about $60.00 at the most and they can save your life! Your local hydraulic supply stores or hydraulic repair shops carry these hose sleeves. Just tell them what size hoses you have and what length hoses you need to be covered.

Do not run any hoses across the front of the press. Keep them to the back and side only. This will help to keep any potential hazard away from you.

Hoses move while operating the press. Make sure they do not rub against anything. Use padding to prevent wear of the hoses.

Designing a press with the cylinder, pump, motor and valve below the hot metal keeps any possibility of a hydraulic fluid cloud lower than your head and provides more safety. But then care must be taken to protect these items from hot scale and hot metal.

If you have a lower cylinder press use trays on the front and back of your press to protect the cylinder and hoses. The back tray should have sides to catch or carry hot scale and hot pieces away from hoses and electric wiring.

The stainless steel front tray on Randy's press

Tray back on Randy's press showing the size and the sides on it

The motor gets hot. Make sure no hoses or electric lines touch the motor.

Have the on/off switch in an easy to reach location on the press in case of an emergency so that you can quickly turn it off.

If you have several people in your shop you may want to have an electric switch lockout to prevent others of less skill/knowledge from using the press. This is another inexpensive safety devise.

Simple commercial electrical switch lock for the press

Have all electrical wiring properly grounded. Wires near the press should be in metal flex conduit for protection from rubbing, burning or shorting out.

Take care in the location and type of foot pedals that nothing can fall on or under them to lock the press in the on or the off position.

Have an oil absorbent material handy if you have a leak or spillage and clean this up before operating the press or the forge as hydraulic fluid is slippery and flammable.

Have a fire extinguisher handy, and the right type for a forging shop.

Have a phone or intercom nearby. So many of us work in a shop alone and if an emergency happens we may not be able to reach a phone or intercom to summon help. Especially if you are a full time smith think about having a personal emergency response system (PERS) that hangs around your neck or on your wrist. These currently run about $40 per month. There are also emergency pendant communicators that tie into your phone system and cost about $300 and have no monthly fees. These could be a life saver, not only in a shop emergency but also in a health emergency.

In a cold shop allow the motor and pump to run with out using the cylinder for at least 10 minutes to warm up the hydraulic fluid. Then operate the cylinder up and down for a couple of minutes without pressure to make sure it's running okay before use.

Personal Safety

Always use safety glasses and perhaps a face shield in operation.

As in all forging wear 100% cotton clothing. No synthetics which melt near flame or high temperatures!

No open top or synthetic shoes.

If you cannot put the mechanicals in another room to move the noise of the motor and pump away from you then earplugs or noise canceling ear muffs are recommended to eliminate hearing loss while operating the press. Once your hearing is damaged it is damaged forever. It will not heal.

Keep hands and fingers from between the dies.

Do ***not*** use Kevlar gloves unless specifically made for hot metal. They can be dangerous! Most types melt at too low of a temperature for forging and will melt onto your skin! They also give one a false feeling of protection.

Know what metal you are working with. This goes for the dies and tooling as well as what you are pressing. Working tool steel until it is cold can harden it which makes it brittle and it can shatter, throwing pieces of metal at you. Do not cool the dies/tooling totally if there is any forging color in them as this can harden them, too. There will be more about this in the tooling section.

Plan what you are going to do with the press BEFORE you actually do it. In operating the press do a cold run first to be sure everything is in place and lined up and that nothing else is in your way before pressing a hot piece.

Focus on all that you do with the press with out distractions. If others are talking with you ask them to wait and then proceed with the press or do it after they are gone. That would probably be safer.

Learn the speed and sounds of your press so that you can recognize if there's a problem and stop the press immediately if a problem is suspected.

Operational Safety

No hand held tools are to be used in the press. They are too long, bend and/or snap too readily and are all around too dangerous.

Never hold a tool in your hand in the press! Only use short tooling that has a handle that is welded to or wrapped around it or hold with a pair of tongs that wraps around the tool. Tooling should be short and stocky. Long tooling can bend and break, throwing shrapnel every where. Handled tools should have a strong connection and strong handles.

Tong handles, hand held tooling handles or bars should never be held with the ends pointing toward the body.

Tongs and other handling tools should be the appropriate length, fit properly, and be in good condition at all times. This will assure that hands and fingers are not exposed when the dies close.

The material that you will be forging should be of the proper length so that the tongs are not in the die area when closed.

Quick change die systems should have a stop in the back and in the front to prevent the tooling plates from flying out of the restraints on an H-frame press.

All tooling and work should be placed in the center of the plates and used vertical or horizontal only. Placing material at an angle can push the piece out of the press at tons of pressure towards you.

In using a hardie/cut-off tool have stops so it can not cut all the way through which would throw the cut off piece like a missile.

Remember that tooling in a press has a lot more contact with the hot metal than in a power hammer and therefore the dies/tooling heat up a lot faster. Remove all dies and tooling using locking pliers or tongs so as not to get burned. Be careful in cooling this tooling. Do not cool it if there is a heat color in the tool as this could harden the tool and make it brittle which would then break the next time you use it.

If any water or wet lubricant remains on the dies, coming in contact with the hot metal will turn this into steam that can spray towards you and burn you.

Be careful not to run your tooling or work into the quick change die holders. This would prevent the easy removal of the tooling.

Only pressing while your metal is hot helps to prevent the metal from flying out of the press. It puts the energy into the hot metal instead of throwing it.

Personally I like plenty of lighting in operating the press. The upper plate casts a shadow as it closes and you need to see where things are in the press. A clamp on safety lamp may be a solution for this problem. Be aware of the wiring and type of light bulb being used in this environment. A heat resistant plastic shield over the bulb area may be helpful to protect it from heat or breakage. I would recommend using a GFCI (ground fault circuit interrupter) safety outlet for this light to prevent you from getting an electrical shock if a problem arises.

Put your tooling away after using it for a job. Do not lay metal and tooling on the floor where you can trip over it or where it could block your foot switch in the open or closed position.

In regards to the safety problem of hydraulic oil that is used in forging presses there is a water based hydraulic fluid that can be used in an industrial setting. Industry likes this as it comes in a concentrated form where you just add water; it is less expensive and is non-flammable and non-toxic to the environment. Besides the safety issue of it being non-flammable there is no disposal problems with the water based product as it is biodegradable.

However, there are major problems for small shops like ours being able to use the water based hydraulic fluid. First off it can freeze. Anti-freeze can be added but then it will be toxic and not biodegradable. There can be a problem with bacterial infestation in your system and the viscosity of the fluid can vary with the water based hydraulic fluid. That can cause damage to your pump and valves. Due to the water in the system this product can cause rusting in your storage tank and in your valves and pump. Dirt from rust can shut down your whole system and parts would have to be replaced instead of cleaned. The pump and valve can be changed to ones made for the water based fluid, but at a higher cost. Even your cylinder should have a bronze clad piston rod to prevent wear between the rod and cylinder walls when using the water based hydraulic fluid. Until they come up with a better product that addresses these issues the hydraulic oil is best for our use.

This information is not all-inclusive on forging press safety, but keep these in mind. There are many dangers that are present in press operation so keep a safety eye open for yourself and for others.

8 Press Maintenance

The press needs to have its oil filter changed after 250 to 500 hours of operation. This depends on how hard you use it. Usually we only operate the press in short increments of about ten minutes. So we may only have actual run time of say an hour or two per day. If that is the case changing the filter every 500 hours should be fine. If you are constantly using the press to punch holes in a line for making railings or gates you may have six hours or so run time per day. Then you may want to change the filter closer to the 250 hour mark. Be aware of the sound your press makes when running. If you hear something different and if you notice that your pressure gauge is acting up by the pressure jumping around, this could be a sign of a clogged filter and maybe that the oil also needs to be changed.

Presses have travel guides that the ram slides in. These should be greased. If you see this grease getting impregnated with scale and dirt, wipe it off of the metal and re-grease the guides. If you don't do this the scale and dirt will start to groove the metal.

I also fully extend the cylinder rod and coat with a light weight oil. I then wipe it off. I do not want so much oil on it that dirt will stick to it and run it back into the cylinder, but enough oil to prevent any rusting. These rods are usually chrome plated to prevent rusting, but I have seen some light rust appear in spots. Also the cylinder does have rubber wipers that prevent dirt from being carried back into the cylinder. I think any piece of machinery works better if it is clean.

Vacuum clean the vents on your motor every month or so. More often if there is welding and grinding being done nearby. This will help to keep the motor cool and increase the motors life. Remember to also grease the motor fittings.

As stated in the safety section inspection of hoses is very important. As soon as you see any wear, especially on the high pressure hoses, replace them.

9 Introduction to Tooling for the Press

I find the key to this machine, as with many others, is tooling. This is only a general description of the tooling I use with simplistic information in regards to heat treating. There will be another chapter explaining their construction and use.

If you are not experienced with heat treating then please take a class in tool making and read my other book, "A Blacksmithing Primer" to get a better understanding of this process. It is not a difficult process, but it needs to be done following the proper steps in order for the process to work as well as for your own safety.

If you do not have the equipment and skills to make your own tooling some of the press and power hammer manufacturers have their own tooling that they sell and will work on the press and they may be open to making custom tooling for you. As the press becomes more popular I am sure we will see more tooling being made for it.

Learning fabrications skills such as electric welding, cutting material, grinding, running a milling machine or lathe can be good skills to learn for this and other projects in your shop. Most vocational schools have day or evening classes for this purpose. It is very important that you know exactly what materials you are using for your tooling. This is so you will know how to heat treat your tooling without it breaking and throwing metal at you in use. For this reason you should stay away from using scrap metal.

Many lower tonnage presses, 15 to 30 tons, use moderate carbon, mild steel for the ram plates and anvil plates with out a problem. I have a 60 ton press and was told that mild steel plates would work as long as I was pushing hot metal. Well, at 60 tons, even with hot metal being used the plates became marked up and grooved and even bent. Some hardening can be done with mild steel by heating thoroughly until it loses its magnetism and quenching in water. No tempering is required and due to the lower carbon should not be in danger of cracking. Even doing this to my plates they still scarred and bent.

I then bought 4140 steel plate for my ram and anvil plates. This is an oil hardening material. Be sure that in hardening this large of a piece of metal in oil that you have more than a five gallon bucket of oil as the oil will heat up fast which can make it flash into flame. Have a solid metal closing lid to suffocate this flame and be prepared with a fire extinguisher and some oil absorbing material. This is a clay absorbent material made for oil spills. The same companies also make kitty litter and this can be of use if no other commercial absorbent is available. Only put the oil in a metal bucket, not plastic. Quenching your hot metal plate heats up the oil enough that it will melt a plastic bucket! This will spill and/or splash hot oil on you and your shop.

Besides your personal burns the oil is easy to ignite in this state which could cause a major fire. Due to this you may only want to do one plate per day and wait for another day for the oil to cool down before quenching another plate. I have been tempering my plates and tooling to a grey color as this is what is done for springs and I want something that has give to it instead of cracking and throwing pieces at me under the pressure of the press.

I recommend that you stamp or somehow mark your tooling and dies with what kind of metal you used for it. Maybe mark your mild steel ones "A36" or "MS" and the tool steel as what type it is such as "1040", "O-1" and so forth before heat treating. This way if and when you have to dress your tools and heat treat them again you will know what liquid to quench them in so that you do not ruin your tooling. Quick change tooling may fit or work better in the top or the bottom guides or have a front or back to the way they fit. In this case you could also stamp your tooling plate with "T" for top tool, "B" for bottom tool and "F" for front of tool if that is helpful for you.

A stamping calling out the material used for this tool

Do not make your tooling any higher than necessary as this takes up your press opening and restricts the size of metal that you can work in the press.

Keep your surfaces smooth and clean of scale. Any marks on your tooling will show up in your work. Then again if you want a rough surface on your work have a rough surface on your tooling.

It is beneficial to have a slight radius on your tooling edges and corners. This will help prevent them from cutting into your work and will make a smoother transition if working down the tooling with the hot metal.

More information on making tooling and using them will be shared later.

Quick Change Tooling

Although a lot of work can be done in the press by using flat anvil and ram plates and hand held tooling, quick change tooling adds another dimension similar to tooling used in the power hammer. Quick change tooling provides a stationary, precision attachment for your tooling which frees up your hands for manipulating the hot metal instead of tooling.

Here is some of the basic tooling to have for your quick change tooling for hot forging on your press:

Flat plates for upsetting, using handled tooling and using dies.

Fullers with flat plate combination for drawing out and flattening.

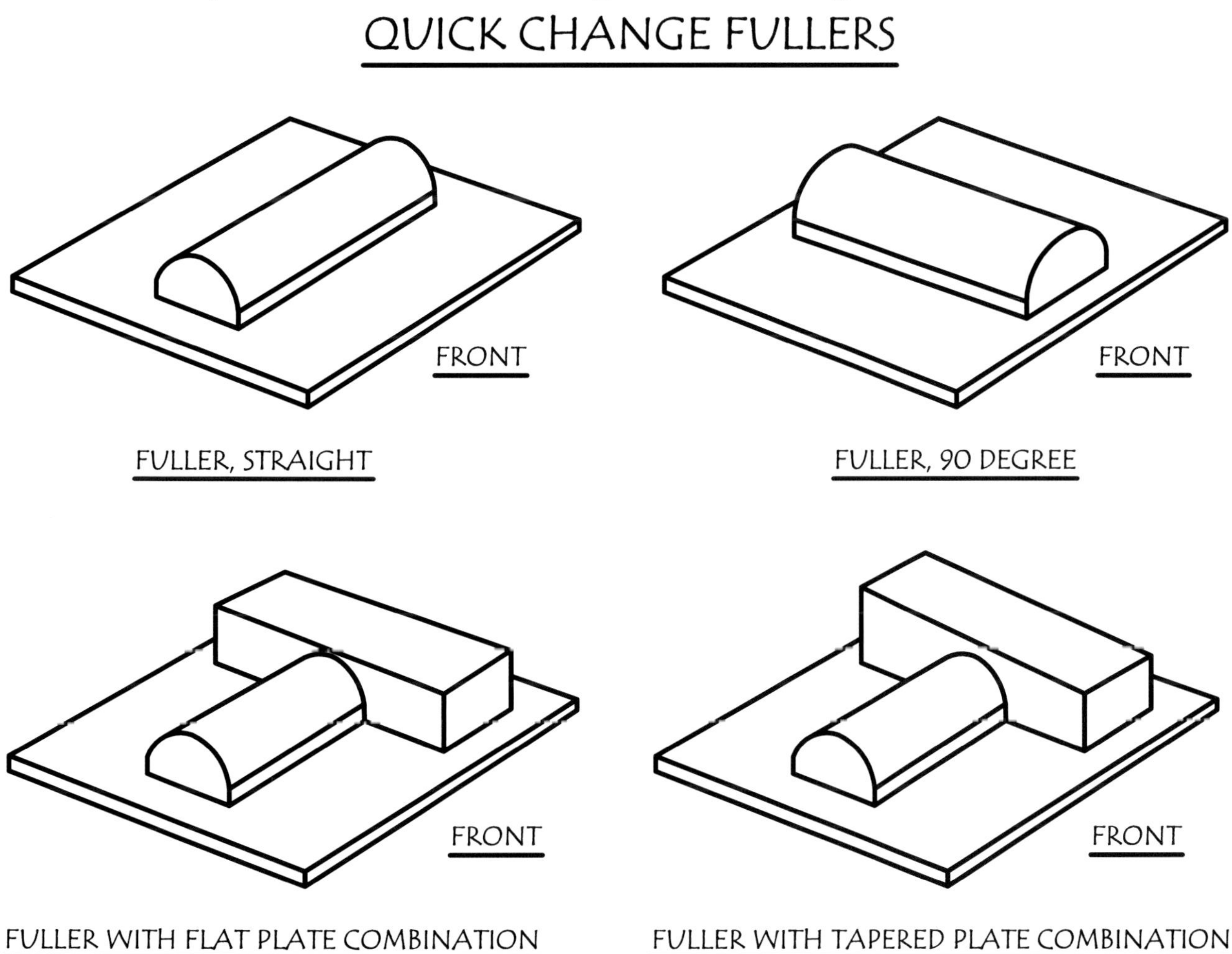

Four types of fuller configurations

Fullers with angled plate combination for drawing out and tapering.

Fullers, straight and ninety degree for drawing out in length and sideways.

Fullers can also be used for bending if you have a double set on the bottom and a single fuller that comes down in the center from the top.

Cut off tool/hardie, usually 3” to 4” wide with stops above the blade so you cannot cut all of the way through your work. This is usually a bottom tool only. I have seen top and bottom cut off tooling, but it is harder to align them in the press so that one is directly over the other. The bottom hardie cuts so fast that there is not much of an advantage in using a top and bottom cutter.

Swages for shaping stock. I have half rounds and v-blocks. Other shapes can be made, too.

Punches, ball end, flat end, round, square or other shapes

Rings. Rings can be used for doing dishing or making bowls using a ball end punch as the top tool.

Rings for forming bowls

All of this tooling can be made in a variety of shapes and sizes depending on what you want to achieve with them. As an example you may have a series of five round end ball punches that are from 3/4 inch round to 2-1/2 inch round.

Die Plates

This is a simple way of producing a detail in your work over and over. These can be used loose by laying them on your anvil plate or welded to quick change tooling plates. If you make your plates over sized just by moving the hot work piece slightly on the die plate changes the design in your work. A lot of the hand held tools I have made were also used to make the designs in my die plates.

These could be texturing dies, embossing dies and forming dies. Texturing dies work from one side and will squish a three dimensional pattern into your metal to add a surface texture or design to it. If you need the design on opposite sides of your work use a die on the top and the bottom. Embossing dies are two dies, a female die that receives the design and a male die that pushes the design into the female die. These were used to make the metal tiles I showed you earlier. Forming dies bend your work to the required shape.

Having the tooling on the top and bottom will increase the work being done and in some instances can give you more forging control as you are working from both sides of your material at the same time.

Handled Tooling

Here is some hand held handled tooling you may want to have:

Handled fullers of different diameters for drawing out and making designs.

Handled square stock and/or flats for cutting in shoulders and making designs.

Handled flats for smoothing work. These have rounded edges.

Handled texturing tooling.

Plus any number of other tools and tool shapes depending on what you want to make.

Hole Punches

If you want to punch holes with your press there are a couple of ways to do this. You can punch all of the way through your work or just push in an indentation for a candle or as a design element. It helps to have a stationery punch in the top plate. This allows the punch to be pushed into your hot piece and to be pulled back out since the cylinder works in both directions.

To prevent the punch from getting stuck in the hot piece I recommend using a forge lubricant such as P3, which is an industrial forge lube or very fine coal dust works, too. Industrial forge lubes come in a concentrated form so you must add water to them to get the right consistency. They are used by slightly heating up your tool and then spraying or brushing the lube onto the tool. You can use a hand held propane torch or the heat from the hot metal to heat up your tooling. When applied the water in the lubricant evaporates leaving a fine powder on the tool which is the lubricant. One application should be all that you need per punch.

In using coal dust I take green coal from my forge and hammer it into a powder. I want it as fine as possible. I then put this dust in a plastic squeezable ketchup or mustard container that I bought at the grocery store. The small nozzle on the end makes it convenient to squirt the coal dust exactly where I want it. Be careful though as it does not take much heat to melt this plastic container. To use this I start punching the hole and after the first partial punch, remove the punch and squirt a little coal dust into the hole before pushing again. Just be careful with the coal dust as when the punch is pulled back out a blast of gas escapes which helps to remove the punch, but gas and dust can be thrown at you.

You can make a round tapered punch to just push part way into a piece of hot metal in order to make a cavity for a candle. This will be a very exacting hole for the size candle that you want to use.

A punch used in the top guides to punch a candle socket

If punching all the way through a piece, instead of just an indentation like in a candle holder, you do it just as you would if you were using a hand hammer and hand help punch. You punch two thirds the way from one side, turn the piece over and punch through over the pritchel hole. The pritchel hole in the press is simply another plate with a hole to support the work as the punch pushes through the hot metal. I use a handled plate so I can slide it under my work when needed.

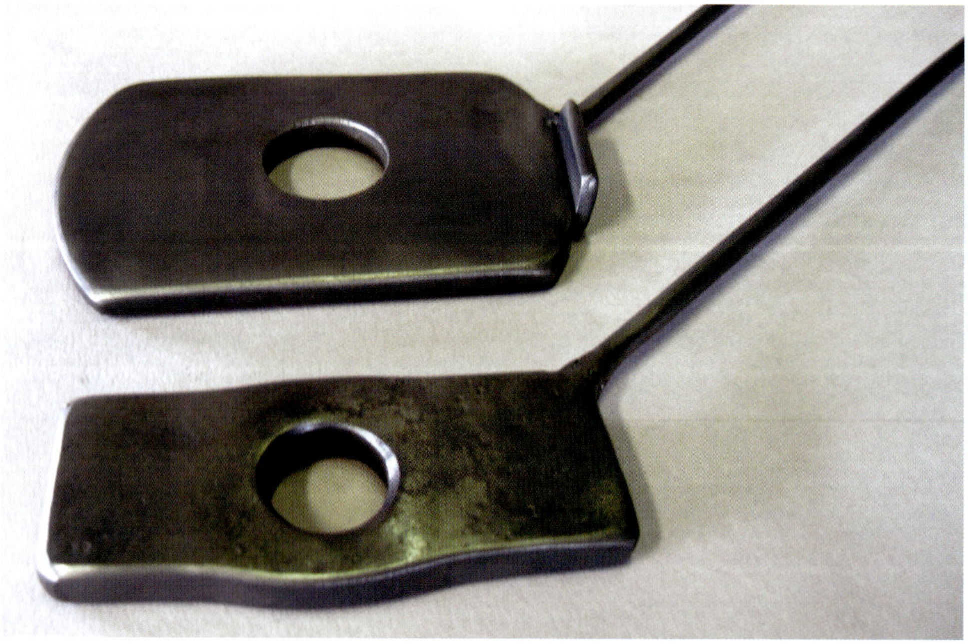

Handled plates used as pritchel holes when punching holes

There are some cases where you want a tapered hole as in a hammer head. A hammer head has a taper from both sides. So your punch is shaped like an eye in a hammer head and it also has a slight taper to it. You punch from one side about two thirds of the way through, turn the hot hammer head over and punch two thirds of the way through that side. Here the plug will drop out on the plate and a hole is not usually needed in your bottom plate.

A hammer eye punch used in exchangeable tooling

The more taper that you have to your punch the more it will distort the material around the hole. This would be like punching a hole and then using larger and larger drifts to make the hole larger. The edges of the hole will become larger than the original bar that you are punching. This is a great detail on gates and fences and other areas where you want the material to bulge out wider than the bar. If you want even more swelling of the punched hole the punch can have a slit chisel shape on the end that then tapers to the finished hole diameter or finished shape. This will start by cutting a slot and then drift out the hole to its finished size in one operation.

For a non tapered hole the shape of the punch may be different than expected. You do not need the taper as you would in a hand operation. Press punches are straight sided as they cut or shear their way through the hot material. This type of punch will shear out the plug. Therefore your bottom plate needs to have a slot that corresponds to the punch and an area below it for the plugs to go. This should be easily removable in order to remove the plugs. This is what is used in the big industrial punching operations and is true on a smaller scale as well.

A stripper plate is very advantageous in punching holes. A stripper plate is a plate that is fixed or hinged horizontally and has a hole in the center of it. It is above the piece that you are punching. When the punch is on the return stroke this plate will hold the hot piece in place and strip the punch from the hot metal. As you need to build a fixture to support this you might as well add other details which will aid you in centering your work or in punching multiple holes spaced evenly in line as in a railing or gate construction. I made my setup on a totally separate plate instead of the quick change system. This gave me more height between the dies. I have bolts on both sides that are used to center the piece to be punched and a stop in the back so that the punch lines up in the same place when the hot piece is turned over to finish the punch through. You may want a plate with a hole in it to slide under the hot piece to act as a pritchel hole for the punch to go all the way through your work depending on what type of hole you are making.

As you see in the photo of my tooling racks I have quite a bit more tooling than mentioned. Each job and each design may need another tool created for it. I also find that once I have made a specific tool for one job I find many other places where it becomes useful.

My tool rack and tool area for the press

Press Fixtures

It seems like any time I say that a press does not have this or that I find an exception to that statement. It is usually the case until I do another job or do some research and find another way to do something another way. Fixtures are an example of this.

Fixtures are used to hold a piece of metal in place while the machine does its operation to it. It holds the metal in a precise location in alignment with the tooling. If you are upsetting a piece vertically in the press as it is being squished down the size of the piece increases horizontally. In that scenario it would be hard to have a tight fitting, clamping style fixture as the hot metal would form over the fixture or push so tight against the sides of the fixture that it would be difficult to remove the work piece. The fixture would also put lines or marks in your work piece. Perhaps that type of fixture would work if the fixture was spring loaded in order to move as the size of the work piece increases in size. Another solution would be to cool off the bottom of the work piece so not to swell into the fixture.

However, fixtures can be used in the press when using hot plate or sheet metal. They may simply be four pieces of square bar stock creating a frame around your work piece and welded to a plate to locate the work piece on center of a die plate or shaping punch. Keep in mind that if you are pushing the plate thinner than its original thickness that the material has to go somewhere and could be drawn out into the sides of your fixture. Pins are another way to locate your work. These make it easier to grab your work for removal when the job is done as there is more open area compared to a solid frame type of fixture.

There will be other solutions and combination tooling shown below that can be used as fixtures to hold your work in place while forging.

Tongs for the press

I often use regular blacksmithing tongs to hold my work at the press. It is important to have tongs that fit the material you are working with as in hand forging. Lately I have been making my own “quickie” tongs for the press and I like them better than blacksmithing tongs. “Quickie” just means that they are fast to make as the jaw to pivot area is simply a twist instead of the three shoulder forged design. What is different about press tongs is that they are shorter than normal forging tongs and stouter. I make them from 1/4 x 1/2 mild steel and the overall lengths of the tongs are around 16 inches long. This is just long enough to reach hot metal in my gas forge and short enough that it is a comfortable length when standing at the press. The pivot is about 8-1/2 inches from the end of the handle. This adds to the power of your grip and allows me to hold larger material.

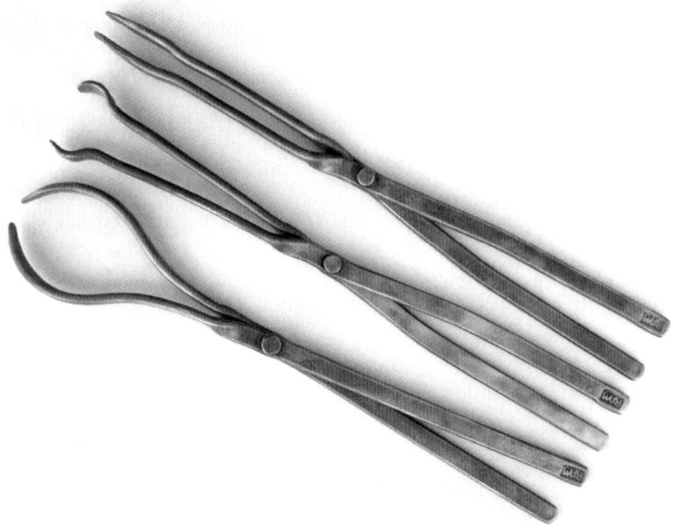

Three pair of quickie tongs I made for the press

I recommend making your own rivets as store bought rivets are made from a softer metal so that you can peen it over while it is cold. Making a mild steel rivet and peening it over hot will last longer and have more strength than the commercial rivets. I also round off the handle ends so nothing sharp is aimed at me in the case that some thing would get pushed in my direction. Due to the shapes and sizes of most of the material that I use in the press I have two types of tongs. These consist of flat tongs and link tongs. I use flat tongs for placing my flat pieces of stock and sheet metal in the press. Link tongs are good for placing stock vertical in the press. These can be in a number of sizes depending on what size stock you are forging.

Once in a while I'll find short handled tongs at the tailgating section of hammer-ins. It is almost like they were waiting for the reins to be welded on. They are usually less expensive than the regular length tongs as there is not as much need for them. These have worked well for me, too, but are harder to find.

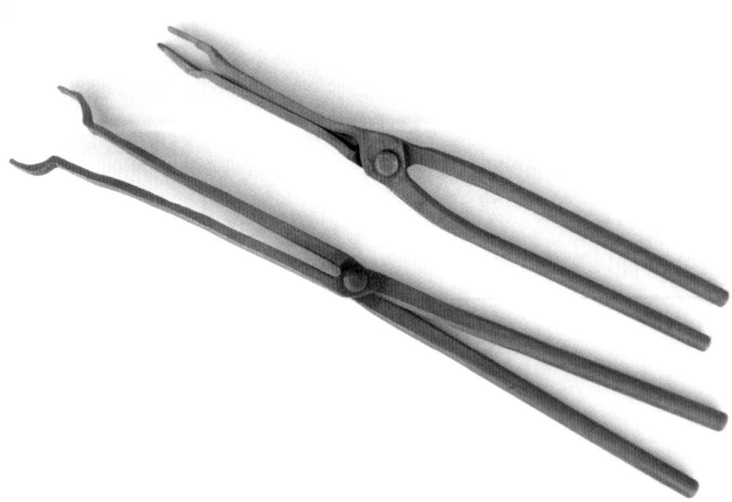

Two pair of short handled tongs that I bought that work well for press work

10 Making Tooling and Dies and How They Are Used

Tool making for the press can be an easy endeavor. If you have any electric welding skills and know how to heat treat metal it can be easy to create what you need for your press. As you have already seen in my photographs I am not a good welder. I use an old tombstone stick welder, but a mig welder would make a prettier job. Still I get good weld penetration in both pieces and I overcompensate with longer welds. My welds may not look nice, but they do hold up.

Be sure that the way your anvil and ram plates attach to your press is very secure and they do not move in operation. Any movement in these plates can put your tooling off center and create an opportunity for breakage of the bolts that hold the plates in place if that is the way they are attached.

The majority of my work is done using quick change tooling and dies. The only problem I have encountered is that I should have made my tool holder guides farther apart. I have times when either my work or my handled tooling will be pushed into the upper tool holders which will bend them closed on the tool, making them very difficult to remove. Therefore it looses the "quick" change tooling designation. If my design in the holders was farther apart and of a heavier construction there would be less chance of having this problem. Changing this design at this point would also mean having to change all of my tooling and die plates. I recently made heavier guides instead of angle iron, but left the distance apart the same.

All of these photographs are of the tooling that I made for my H-frame press. Tooling for a C-frame press may be turned ninety degrees from what you see here due to the way you use that type of tooling. In these photographs of the quick change tooling the long side is the front of the tool.

When I first started making tooling for my press I bought a bar of 1/2 inch x 4 inch wide hot rolled mild steel to use for the base plates for my quick change tooling. I would cut this to length to fit my tool holders and use a flap disc sander in my 4-1/2 inch body grinder to slightly radius all edges. If you have sharp edges in your tooling or plates they may have a tendency to cut into your anvil and ram plates. I also radius the corners of the plates as it is easier to hit the inside of the tooling guides with a curve than a sharp corner. I would cut up the whole bar, grind and would heat up each plate in the gas forge until it lost its magnetism and then quickly quench it in water while swishing it around. I use the gas forge as it is easier to get an even heat on the whole plate and I get less scale on the plate, too. This hardens the plate, but not to a point where it is anywhere near brittle so no tempering is needed. I would then use a wire wheel cup brush to clean any scale that remains on the plate. I would now have a stack of these plates ready to go and do not have to stop to make a plate when making a new tool. Currently I get these plates laser cut to size. In doing quantities of these at a time it is less expensive than buying that size bar and having to cut each piece. All I have to do is sand/grind the edges and harden.

So now I use these plates to make my quick change tooling as shown next. Any time I say "plate" this item is usually what I mean.

Fullers

Three fullers used in the press

Fullers can be made by welding a piece of round bar to a plate. Smaller fullers will cut deeper into your hot work. Larger fullers will cut less yet still push the metal along but without deep grooving of your material.

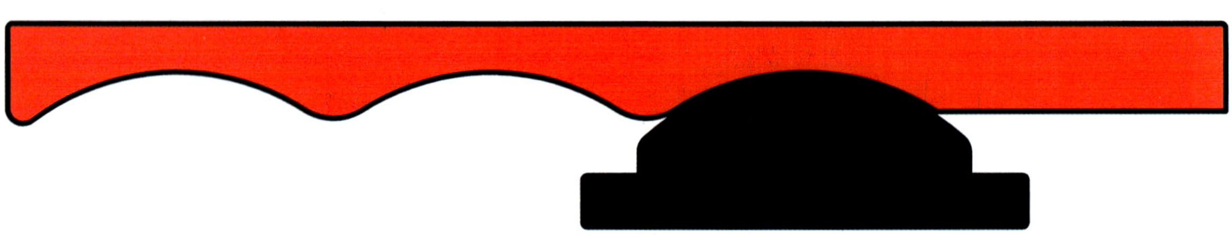

A larger fuller will have less problems with transition in drawing out

There may be instances where both will be of use for you. Most of the fullers that I make are out of moderate carbon steel that I just harden as I did the plates. After time you may see them scaring and getting marks in them, especially if you have a higher tonnage press. If that is the case you may want to use a tool steel for the material for the fuller, but I still use it on the moderate carbon plate. This is true of most of my tooling. If you are working bronze all of the time then mild steel may be fine for most of your tooling, but forging steel will probably require tool steel tooling.

For my setup I cut the round stock to 1-3/4" shorter than the plate. This gives room for the quick change tooling guides that the plate slides into and room for the welding so it will not interfere with the guides. Your spacing may be different. I grind the ends of the bar to a 1/8 inch radius or so to help prevent sharp edges from cutting into my work if it overlaps the end of the tool. I do the heat treating of the round stock before welding it to the plate in most instances. For mild steel, moderate carbon steel, I do it the same way I did the plate. For tool steel I heat treat this by hardening it and then heating the whole piece until it has gone through all of the tempering colors and is grey as in making a spring. I want it to be tough but not brittle at all. Be sure you know which tool steel that you are using so that you quench it in the right liquid for hardening. I like 4140 because it is very strong and tough and less likely to be brittle or crack. This should be quenched in oil for hardening to maintain this toughness. Quenching 4140 in water can make it crack and/or be too brittle for press work. You may find other tool steels that work well for this application.

A normal fuller goes from the left to the right on your plate so that it is ninety degrees to your work as it is being fed over the fuller. A ninety degree fuller is just that, it runs from the front to the back of your plate and is in line with placing your work over it. A fuller makes your work longer where the ninety degree fuller will make your work wider.

A 90 degree fuller will make your work wider

It is important to center the tool on the plate. Centering your tooling properly with all of your tooling will make sure that top and bottom tooling will align properly.

Usually I weld all around the tool to the plate. I want a substantial mount, not something that could crack or come loose. I do not worry about the welding heat ruining the heat treatment of the tool. I have never had the welding heat get so high on the tool that it has even gotten to the grey tempering color. You could wire wheel the tool and watch the surface colors while welding if you have any concern with this. Once done welding I clean up the weld and make sure there is no splatter on the plate that could interfere with the plate sliding into the guides. Some times welding causes the plate to warp just enough that it will not fit back into the quick change guides. If this is the case I either use a belt sander or a flap disc to grind the plate until it will again fit into the guides. Usually it is the bottom center of the plate that requires grinding.

I should mention that this same process is what is done with most of my tooling so in further discussions of making press tooling just refer back to this information.

That is it! Now you have your first tool for the press.

The fuller can be used for drawing out a bar to make it longer or wider, to make a decorative element or used for bending if used in conjunction with a double fuller which is really a bending tool not a fuller. In drawing out you want your metals fullering marks to overlap as you work down the bar so that you do not get thin pieces of stock pushing out in between.

It is important to space your fullering marks so that you do not get thin pieces of metal in between

If you do not overlap where the fuller pushes on your stock and you get thin material in between those areas it could easily fold over creating areas that later could crack or splinter. As in hand forging you fuller down the bar and then use the flat face of the hammer to flatten it back out. To do this on the press it is handy to have a combination tool of a fuller and flatter.

The fuller/flatter combination for top and bottom tooling

The fuller is shorter than previously shown and has a square or rectangular bar ninety degrees from the fuller. With this combination, you fuller your work several times down the bar and then place it on the flatter to keep everything in line and to squish your high areas back into the bar. Care must be taken in squishing on the fuller as it is easy to go all of the way through your hot bar. You want to do this gradually and at the same depth as you work down the bar.

If you are drawing out tapers you may want your flatter to have an angled surface. This angle would be similar to your finished taper on your bar. It does not take much of a taper to achieve what you need in your tapering.

Side view of the taper die showing that it does not take much of an angle

You can also make two angled plates for drawing out tapers without having a fuller. Using a top and bottom tapering tool is much like using angled blows with your hammer. As you draw out a taper in one direction the material will spread wider, too, so turn your work ninety degrees before it spreads too far and work in that direction back and forth until you have drawn it out to a point. My tapering tool is about 3 inches wide so I can use it for any size material that I want to work with.

I have had people say that a power hammer works faster than a press. It all depends. With the right tooling, such as this fuller and flatter combo, and depending on the size of bar you are working, I have drawn out pieces faster on my press than I could do on my air hammer and it was also easier on me.

If you want a decorative element a top and bottom fuller can be used. Squishing from both sides at once pushes most of your material forward, but a slight amount will make a rounded area to either side at the same time. Your next squish should be past this area and just repeat down the bar. This puts the design of the fullers on both sides plus you have the rounded areas highlighting the design. Doing this on a tapered bar gives a slightly different effect.

Decorative bars made with only top and bottom fullers

Bending can be done by having two pieces of round bar spaced a distance apart to allow the upper fuller and the stock you want to bend go in between them. This would be your bottom tool.

Lower bending tooling

The top tool is a fuller. Be careful in doing this cold as all of your force is spread out between your tooling and the piece that you want to bend. This is harder on your tooling and so it is imperative that you have good material and good welds for this to hold up. It pushes not just downward on your bending tool but also outward so it could break the front piece off towards you.

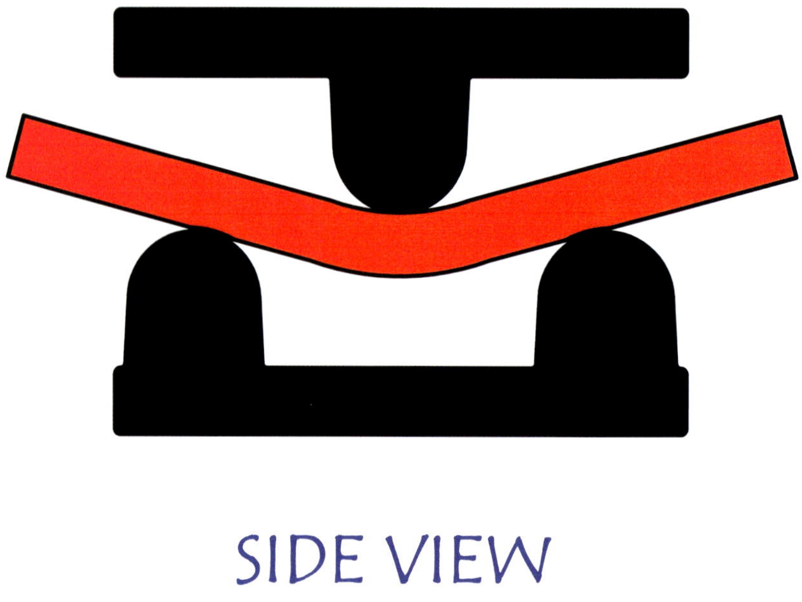

Side view of bending tool alignment

I've done this with the bar hot and it does work, but you also have the probability that you will push some of the tooling into your hot bar to some degree. I needed a tight bend in some 2 inch round bar and I had tried hot bending it using a heavy duty bending fork in the leg vise and a big, three foot long handled fork to no avail. Even with that leverage it just did not move. The press did a good job of it and the marks became part of the design.

Set Tools

Set tools are used for cutting shoulders into your work. They work like the edges of your anvil with half faced or edge hammer blows. By having a square or rectangular piece of steel welded to your plate a flat top plate can push shoulders into your work. You may want your tool to have one half of the bar with a radius on the edge and the other half of the bar with a sharp edge depending on if you want a fillet in your finished shoulder to give it more support or not. A sharp inside corner on a shoulder has more of a chance of breaking at that point. Having top and bottom set tools can be used for making tenons.

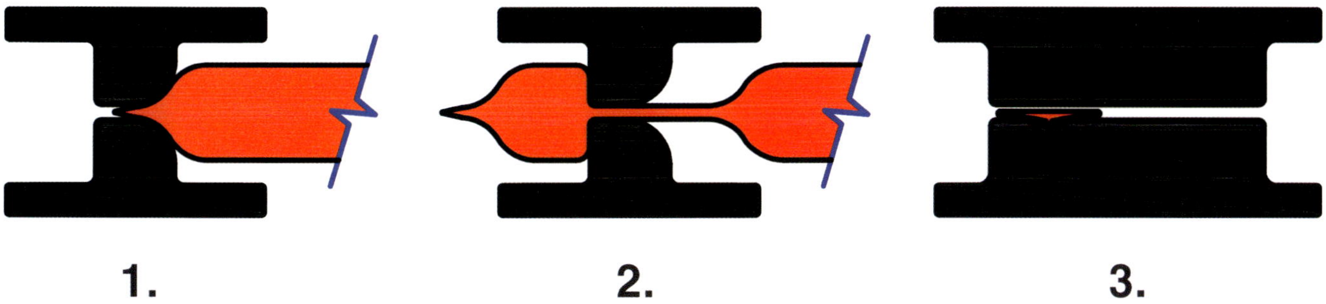

Tooling and steps for forging a leaf

You can make set tools for special projects. An example would be for forging out leaves. The front shoulders of your top and bottom tools would have a large radius for shaping the point of your leaf. The top of the tools would be flat for flattening your work and the far edges would have just a slight radius for cutting the back of the leaf to the stem and for drawing out your stem. You could also file or grind a very low profile "V" shape on top of your lower tool to press in the taper of the sides of your leaf and to press in the center vein.

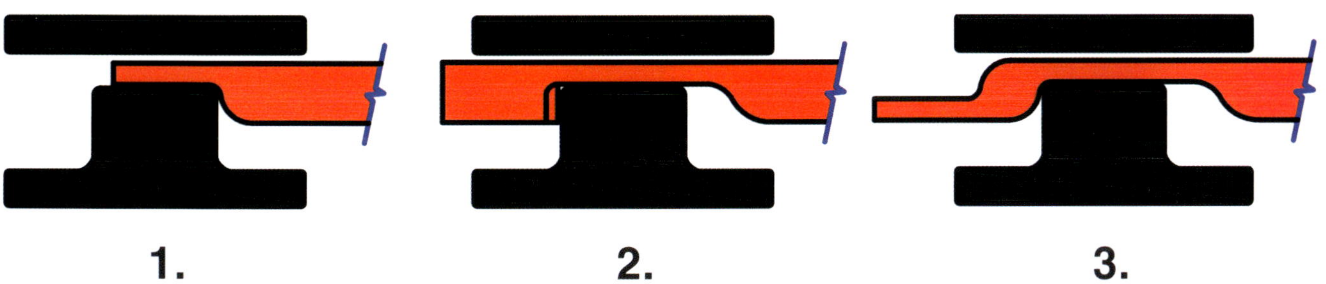

Tooling and steps for forging a tong jaw

A similar set up can be done in order to forge out tong jaws. In this instance you would just need a flat plate on top and a bottom shoulder or set tool. This tool would have the front and back edges slightly rounded. The top of the tool needs to be deep enough for the boss or area of your tongs where the hole will go. You will make the tong jaw just as you would on the anvil. The first step would be to cut in the shoulder and spread the area for the tong jaws. This is done on the front side of your set tool. The second step is a ninety degree counter clockwise turn of your piece and about a thirty degree angle to your tool and squish again. Finally another ninety degree counter clockwise turn of your piece and place your work past your tooling the same distance as the width of the boss area. This will cut in the last shoulder and then you can start drawing out the reins.

You can use a top and bottom tool for shaping the tong jaws. You just need the outside shape of the jaw on the lower die and a positive shape on the upper die. As an example the lower tool could have a "V" cut into it that is the outside dimension of your tong jaw and the upper tool would have a "V" shape coming out of it the size of the inside of your tong jaw. So it would be like a chisel pushing into a "v" swage. You can do this to any size or shape that you want.

You can do this to shape the tongs as in making bolt tongs. You would need a cut out in the lower tool that matches the final shape that you want for the tong jaw with the inside corresponding shape on the top tool that will push into the lower die and form your tong half.

Punches

Punches can be used for making holes, either all the way through a piece or part way through. They can also be used for forming as if you were pushing your thumb down the side of a block of clay. Two types of punches are the flat end and round or ball end.

Flat top punches

Round end or ball end punches

These can also be straight sided or tapered. These can be round or square or any shape that you want. They can easily be made by starting with material of the shape and size that you want. I like using a small lathe to turn them if I want a taper or ball end, but you can get pretty close to the form that you want by using a flap disc on a body grinder. The nice thing about a flap disc is that with more pressure you can remove more material and then with lighter pressure you can finish it off to remove the grind marks and have a pretty smooth surface. Just remember that any marks on your tooling will be marks in your work. Also make sure your punch is long enough to punch deep enough for what you are doing yet is not so long that you can not get your work under it. As in the edges of the fullers I also radius the edges of my flat end punches.

An advantage of turning your punches on a lathe is that you can also create a center punch nipple in the exact center of your punch.

Round tapered punch used in exchangeable tooling.
Note the center punch nipple

This helps in locating the punch in your work. If you center punch your work as to where you want the punched hole to be this can be used to locate the punch on your work. Again heat treat and then center your punch in the plate and weld all around.

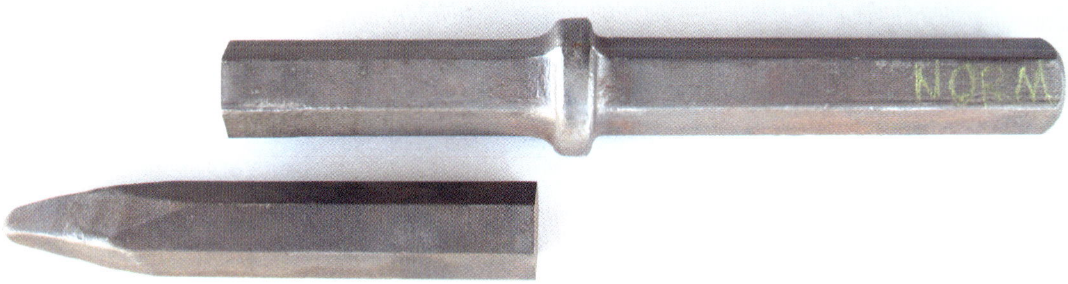

Jack hammer bit used for making tooling.

I use jack hammer bits for most of my punches and created a holder so that I can exchange them easily and quickly. I like the jack hammer bits because they have a collar that can be used for pushing and pulling the punch. I have found jack hammer bits at scrap yards and from smiths that sharpen them. Once they get too short for road work they are usually thrown away or scrapped and I can get them for free or at scrap steel pricing. They are still long enough for punch tooling.

In order to fit the tooling holder I make sure that all of my bits are the same size as they come in a multitude of sizes. I normalize the jack hammer bit so it is soft enough to cut with a band saw and to turn on a lathe. I do this by slowly heating until it is a low orange and letting it air cool on a fire brick. I usually mark the tool with "NORM" using a colored pencil so that I know that it has been normalized and I do not have to do it again in making a different tool. Once it is cold I cut it off in the band saw to the length that I need for the tool, leaving the handle end intact. Once that is done I can either turn it in a lathe or forge out the end to the required size and shape. Then I use a band saw to cut the handle end off right behind the collar. The collar on the jack hammer bit serves as the support when pushing and the holder when pulling.

Interchangeable punch holder. I pieced the tool holder together in layers by cutting several pieces and welding them together. The opening is wider than the thickness of the collars and the hinge closes to lock the hex bar securely in place. I think you will understand more from my photos of this tool then me trying to explain it any further.

Punch holder parts for construction

Exchangeable tooling holder open to receive tooling

Punch slid into holder opening

Tool holder closed to hold punch

A stripper plate would be advantageous for separating your punch from the hole but stripper plates also make it hard to see where the punch is located on your work. You have to decide what to use depending on the circumstances. If you do not use a stripper plate you need to punch a little at a time. Punch and remove, punch deeper and remove again. Before it starts sticking in the hole use a forge lube or fine coal dust and punch and remove again. I've had times where the punch stuck and I was using a hammer and even a crow bar to pry it loose. I got it out, but I marked up my work, too. Sometimes this happens when I get too anxious instead of being patient. Punching a little at a time and then removing the punch does help.

I should mention that while we are doing this punching that the punch is in constant contact with our hot piece of metal and is absorbing a lot of heat. This is true with all of the press tooling and dies. It may not have any forging color to it, but it IS HOT!!! If you are doing a lot of punching you may want to remove the punch from the guides and cool it off some, but not all of the way. Use tongs for handling the punch!

I do not like to use handled tooling for punching holes. When this is done you would have a bolster plate, a thick plate or bar with a hole all of the way through it, underneath your work and a handled punch over your work. The problem here is aligning these two tools so that you do not chip off the edge of your punch or the edge of the bolster hole with either tool and make a mess of your hole at the same time. You do not have the beginning or marking of the punch starting on the bottom of your work as you would have with a hammer and hand held punch on the anvil so there is nothing to guide where to place your punch on the opposite side.

An example of what can be done with a ball end punch

I like to think of my ball punches as my thumb or finger tips and push it into the top edges of a block of hot metal and let it peel a piece of the block down the side. Careful in doing this! It could raise up the other side of the block and even throw it. The key is to keep it hot and use a pair of tongs to try to hold it flat on the anvil plate. Make sure your tongs are not as wide as your work is high so they are not in the way of the press or the punch. Keeping your work hot puts most of the presses energy into the work instead of moving it in another direction.

Stripper Plates for Punch Tooling

I have already explained how a stripper plate works, but there are a few ways to make them. One way is a non-adjustable item by its self simply on a plate.

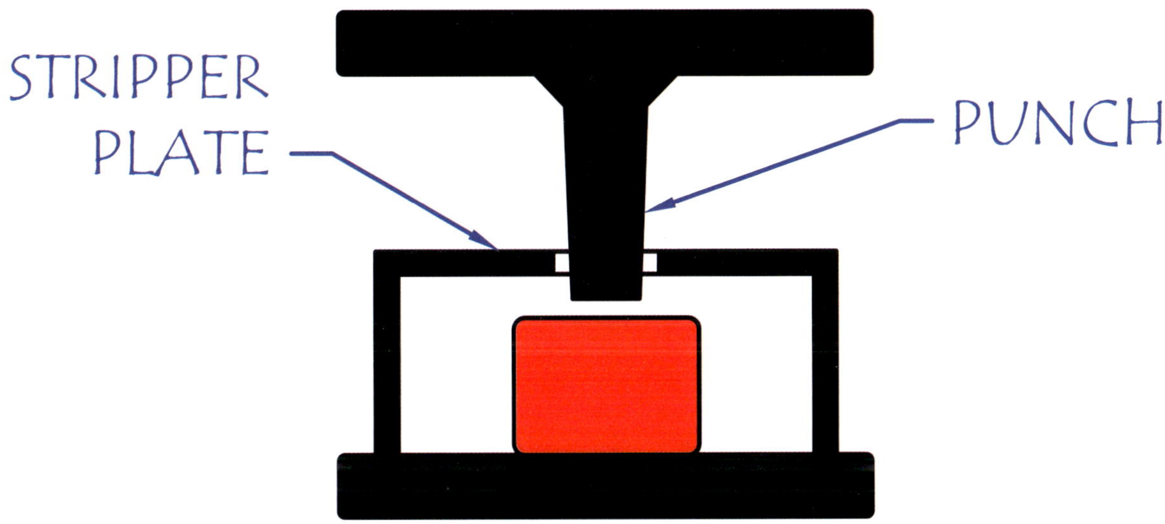

A simple three sided stripper plate

It could be a three sided opening with two vertical plates and a horizontal plate on top of them. The horizontal plate would have a hole in the middle for the punch to go through. The vertical plates would be welded to the anvil plate or even to a quick exchange plate depending on how wide a piece you are putting in this arrangement. In using any of these stripper plates your work will be hot when punching so the plate still may put a slight flat area on your work as the punch is pulled out and the work piece is pulled up against it.

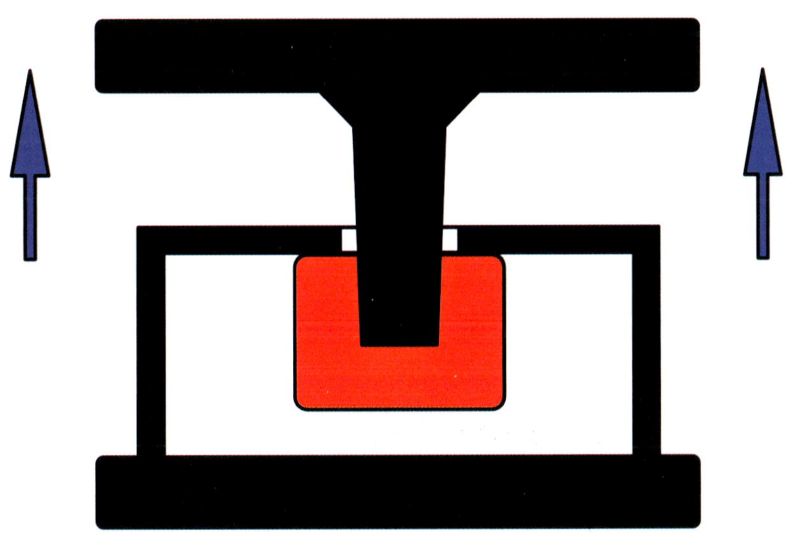

Stripper plate showing the work piece raised up in removing the punch which then strips the punch from the work piece

As it is hard to see where the punch is located as it comes down I thought of another design in making a swinging stripper plate with slots cut into it. One end of the plate would pivot horizontally on a bolt. One slot would slide over a bolt opposite from the pivot and another slot from the center hole where the punch would have gone into your work. This way you could start the punch into your work with the stripper plate open so you can see and position your work under the punch. Then once you are ready to remove the punch you can rotate the stripper plate over the work piece and pull out the punch.

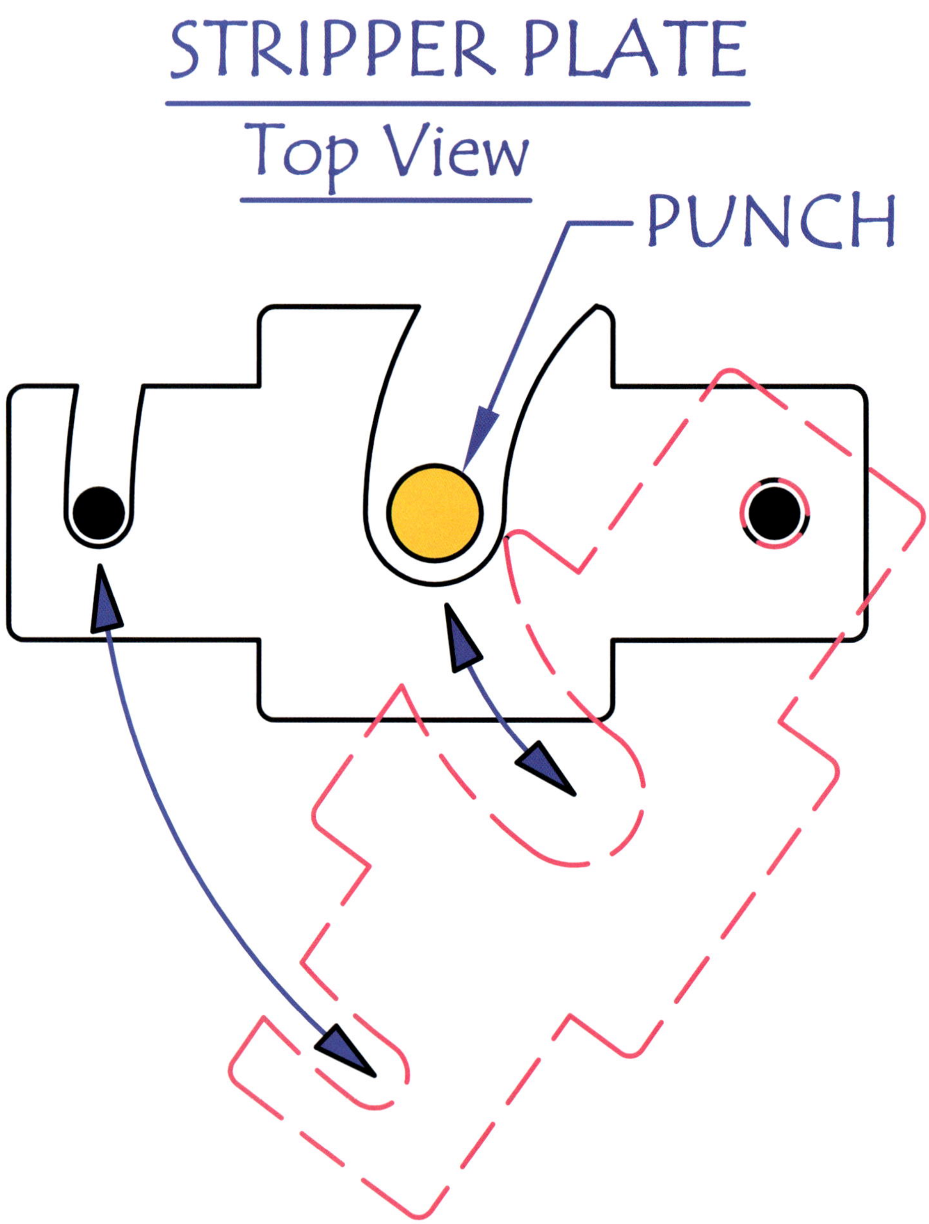

Rotating stripper plate

The other type of stripper plate is an adjustable one.

Adjustable stripper plate on a bar positioning plate.
Stripper plate partially open

Instead of using pieces of flat bar or plate for the vertical sides, heavy all thread is used. The stripper plate has two holes to go over these all threads and a hole in the middle for the punch. Nuts and washers are used below and above the plate in order to raise or lower the plate to the thickness of what you are punching and to secure it in place. As it is hard to see where your work piece is due to the stripper plate being over it, it may be helpful to have a stripper plate that will swing out of the way when aligning your work and swing closed when punching. This can be done by making one of your attachment holes that goes over the bolts be a curved slot that goes between one of the bolts.

Top view. Stripper plate totally open, bar in place and stop located
on end of bar

The longer this plate extends over your work the less chance there is of it marking your work piece when it is drawn up against it when the punch is removed. I also like to round off any edges to help in this, too.

Horizontal bolts on both sides of your plate can be used to adjust the location of your work on center and for equal spacing of multiple holes,. This will be an adjustable fixture. You will need vertical bars with tapped holes spaced equally on either side of the center of your plate and two bolts in each bar. This has to fit under the area for your stripper plate. Make sure that your bolts are far enough apart on the vertical plates that there is room for the punched hole to swell open with out coming in contact with the bar or the bolts.

Stripper plate removed to show the bar positioning arrangement

When I set up to use this arrangement I take a short sample bar of the size bar I will be punching and scribe a line down the exact center. This is a cold piece. I then center punch exactly on center at either end of the bar. Using the punch that has the center punch nipple on the end I move the sample work piece under the punch until it sets into the center punch mark on one end. Then tighten up the side bolts on the sample piece but not so tight that it will not slide through. Now slide the piece and see if the second center punch mark lines up or not. If not then adjust your bolts until it does. Keep sliding the sample piece back and forth adjusting the four bolts until the punch lines up with the center punch marks at both ends of your sample. You are close, but this still will not work as this is a cold piece and the hot piece will be slightly larger. So heat up the sample piece and equally open the bolts until it will fit in the opening left by the bolts. Now you are ready to punch.

Test piece centered in place with back stop located on end of bar

The next thing that can be helpful is a back stop or a spacing guide depending on if you are just punching one hole or a series of them. Again doing things hot causes your work to be larger so your guides should be set when your work is hot. To make an adjustable back stop fabricate a four sided open ended box that a small piece of square bar will slide in and out. Have a threaded hole in the top of the box and use it for a bolt or thumb screw to lock the bar in position. As this box will be located off center from the punch the bar will need to be bent at ninety degrees to make an "L" and then that bent at a forty-five degree so it lines up close to center of the material coming through the bolt guides on your adjustable guides and stripper plate. You can also slide another bar over the first one that will lock in place. As an example of its use, in making a hammer and punching out the eye you will punch from one side and then you want to turn it over and punch from the other side. After punching about two thirds of the way through slide the back stop up against the back of the hammer head and lock in place. Remove the punch, turn the hammer head over and slide it until it his the back stop. Now the punch will line up exactly with the bottom hole and make a perfectly aligned hole.

Top view. Test piece in place, stripper plate closed, back stop locked in place

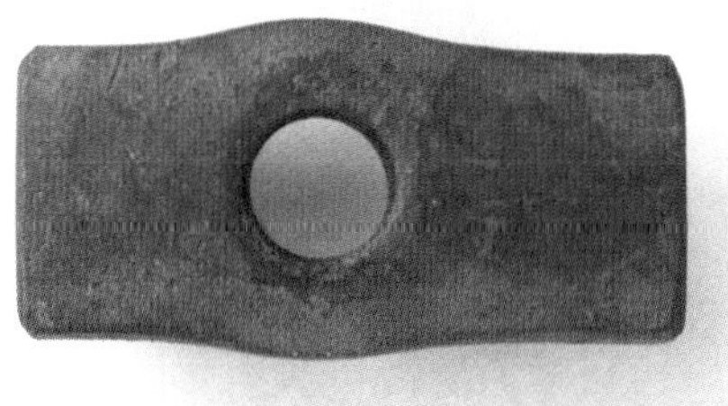

An example of a hole punched using the stripper plate and bar positioning tooling

How do you know when you are two thirds or whatever depth you want the punch to be in your work? You can gauge it by eye by following the end of the punch as it comes down. Even though you can not see the end of the punch once it enters your work still keep your eye on where you think the end of the punch is as it moves down and stop the press when it gets to the depth that you want. Another way is to mark your punch with chalk or colored pencil at the exact depth that you want it to go. Then stop the press and pull the punch back out when it reaches that mark.

If you want to do multiple holes in a bar you can make another back stop that is bent so it goes over the bar instead of hitting the end of it. Now make a separate "L" spacer bar that one end will fit in a finished hole that has a bar welded to it that is horizontal and the right length to hit the back bar to give you the correct spacing between holes. The nice thing is if you cut the horizontal bar too short you can still slide out the back stop to give you the length that you need between holes.

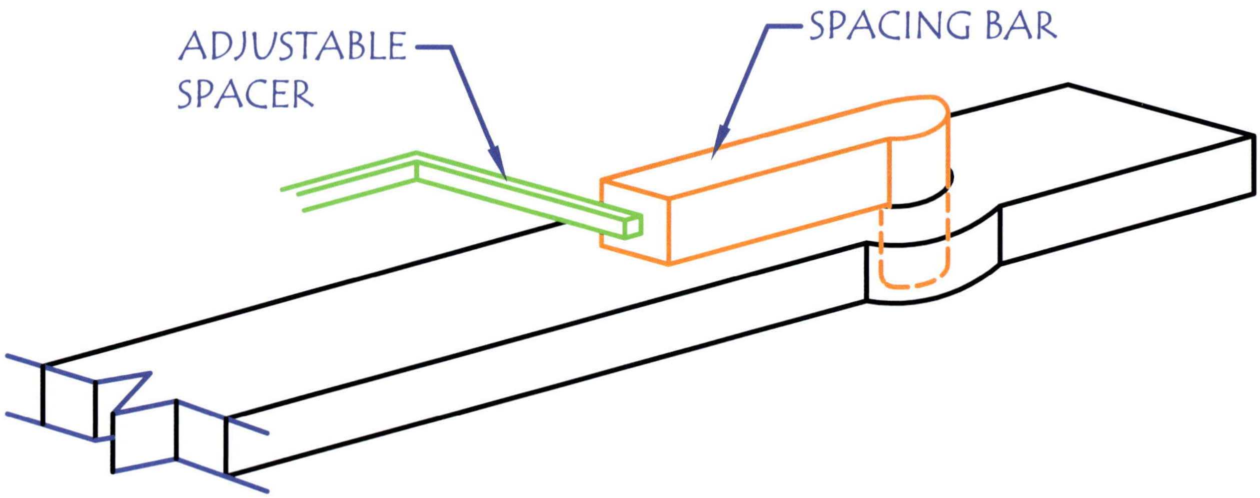

Space bar used against back stop to locate multiple hole punches

The only awkward part here is that you have to remove the piece from each hole and relocate it in the hole that was just finished and the press is in the way. If you can pull the work piece forward to do this it will work okay. If not you will have to go around the press to relocate the spacer bar into the last hole. In this case a C-frame would be easier to use than an H-frame unless you can come up with a spacer that can be used from the front of the press. I have also seen presses designed mainly for punching that allow the hot metal to run from left to right instead of front to back. This was similar to a C-frame press but with a much wider anvil plate to support your work in punching. This was a great solution that allows you to see where your hole will be located and for moving or adjusting back stops or spacing tooling.

Embossing/Shaping/Forming Dies

These usually require a top and a bottom tool. The bottom tool receives the shape that you need and the top tool pushes the metal into that form. If you want to make a wavy bar the tooling could be several pieces of round bar welded to the plates. They are spaced far enough apart to receive the opposite round bar tooling plus three times the thickness of the material you want to squish or more. You may have three bars on the top tool that push into the center spacing of two bars on the bottom tool. With this arrangement you can put waves in a bar in just one push or keep feeding the hot bar through the tooling and do the whole bar and in one heat!

Tooling for making bowls comes under this category. This could be a thick ring on the bottom tool and a large diameter, ball end punch for the top tool. You will have to practice with different configurations to see what works best for the size, thickness and depth that you want to achieve for your bowl. Have more than enough spacing between the tools when they close as it can very difficult to remove a bowl in the bottom die if this is not taken into consideration. Using a flat bottom punch will seat the bottom of your bowl flat on the anvil plate so the bowl sits flat when done. Careful not to push the bowl if there is too much resistance as this punch could tear through the bottom of your material.

You can also use this configuration for drawing out a bowl shape.

Top and bottom bowl tooling for drawing out the material and shaping into a bowl

The top tool is about 2-1/2 inches round with a ball end, and heat treated and welded to your plate. This can be used to make your bottom tool. I heat up a block of steel that corresponds to this sizing, lay a piece of cold annealed sheet metal the thickness of what you will be squishing on top of the hot block and squish the ball end tooling into it. The sheet metal will give you the spacing that you need between your tooling and the top tool will form the bottom tool to match it perfectly. If you will be working heavier than 1/8 inch material you may want to heat up your sheet metal enough that it will form to the shape of the top tool and still have strength to push into the bottom block. I then take the flap disc and round off the inside sharp line that has been created in the bottom tooling and the outside line of the tool. This allows you to move your work between the tooling instead of sinking it into one spot as you did in the bowl tooling above. Then you can use this tooling to draw out the thickness of the plate you are working with and dish it at the same time.

Remember the iron tiles and the sea shells I referred to earlier? Both of those were made with a top male die and a bottom female die, otherwise known as embossing dies. I would have loved to have spent a month with the smith that made the metal tiles I showed you earlier to learn some of his knowledge on making those dies! As can be seen in his finished tiles the dies were all hot forged. I am still looking for information as to how those dies were made so that I can do it with that precision. Since that is not possible we have to re-learn the techniques that were used or combine those with some modern techniques.

Tooling I made to forge steel sea shells. The one tool was used to push in the shells' ribs in the bottom die

I started by doing a lot of stock removal in making the dies for the sea shells. I ground large thick plates to be close to the size and curvature that I needed using my four and a half inch body grinder. The top tool looks like the finished shell, but is actually the inside shape and surface of the shell. Most of the detail was put in using a flap disc sander to remove the material between the ribs of the shell. I then heated this die and used hand held tooling on the anvil to remove any grind marks and to create the surface texture and final detail in this die.

The bottom tool is the swage that the metal gets pushed into creating the shape, texture and detail of the outside of the finished shell. This took a lot of grinding to make this shell bowl. I kept using the top die to make sure it fit in the bottom die with the right depth and curvature of the top die. Once this was close to what I needed I made a handled tool to cut in the exterior ribs of the shell into the bottom die. This tool was as long as the shell was high and the edge was the same curve as the shell. It tapered to a flat edge along that curve. It was similar to a curved knife blade. I heated up the bottom die and using the press pushed the dull knife into it to create the ribbing in the swage. I tried to line them up with the upper die ribbing so the upper tool would push the shell material into the ribs of the bottom tool. The top edge of the bottom tool has a slight recess ground into it to hold the laser cut steel blank in position. This makes it a fixture and a forming die.

I have three sixteenths thick steel laser cut to fit this tooling, it is then heated and squished into the dies. Due to the shells overall size it takes several heats to obtain the detail that I want in the finished sea shell.

The inside and outside of a finished sea shell using the press dies.

Considering what I had to work with in both knowledge and tooling I am happy with the end result. When pressed in this tooling sea shells do come out of it. Now in only making a few sea shells the time put into making these dies would have been frivolous, but in making twenty-five or more the tooling will pay for itself.

Spring Tools

Spring tools are also useful in the press. I have used these as hand held and as bottom tooling for quick change tooling so that I do not have to hold them. Here are some more forming tools using springs:

A spring tool for quick change tooling used to make an acorn

Another type of shaping die is for doing a form either on the end of a bar or in the center of a bar. I have made tooling for producing acorns, balls and centers for newel posts. You need your pattern or positive part to start. You can turn an acorn or a ball on the lathe to what ever size you want or do them by forging and then sanding and filing to sharpen up any detail that you desire. This needs to be welded to a round stock handle that is about 8 inch long or more. The handle should also be about a quarter of the diameter of the end design without being flimsy. Clean up the weld as much as possible and have a nice transition into your piece.

Next get two blocks of steel that are each about the same thickness as the overall thickness of the final part and at least twice the width and length of your part to use as your top and bottom dies. Keep the acorn or ball or whatever design piece cold as you push it into the center of the hot bottom block about one quarter of the way into it. This way you can see where the pattern is on your block and it will line up better when you are using both die blocks. Remove the pattern and cool it off. Now heat up the bottom die and top die plate, place the cold pattern into the lower block, put the top block on center above it and squish. If your pattern is large you may want some lubricant on the pattern and not close the press on it all at once, but close some, open a little, turn the pattern and then close again, open the press, remove and cool off the pattern and then return to the blocks and close again. Sometimes I add sides or guides on one of the die plates so that they line up in pressing in the pattern. I do not weld them to the plates first because if you do you have to heat up the die and plates and in squishing the pattern in between them even the plates will be forged down and out which will expand in your guides and be very difficult to remove.

After forming the die blocks I let them normalize. Once cold I place the pattern in the bottom die block and put the upper die block on top of that and clamp together so every thing is lined up. If I did not use the side guides on the block this is where you can grind the sides of the upper block to align with the lower block. Now you may want to weld on back and side guides to keep them lined up in forging. I then heat treat the dies and just weld the lower die block to a plate to slide into the quick change tooling guides. This is because instead of welding these dies to top and bottom plates I will make a spring handle to help to align the blocks and to pull them apart while forging. These springs are moderate carbon/mild steel, not tool steel. Just by hardening and tempering the bend area on the handle I get years of use out of them and have no problem with breakage. Make sure that the spring is long enough and low enough on the die so it will not hit the anvil or ram plates in operation.

The same process is used for center of the bar die plate designs. The only difference is the pattern goes through the front and the back of the blocks.

Top and bottom die plates after the master piece was pushed into them

View from the back of the press showing the spring tooling.
You can also see the alignment guides on the sides of the bottom die.

Here are the center bars made with the previous tooling.
There are two pieces per bar.

This die set was created so I could do one center bar on either end of the bar. This produced two center bars that were then cut off and welded to the appropriate size material.

In using these die blocks the main concern it that you are putting the right size material into them to forge out the end result. If the material is too large you will get overlapping of the material as you work around the piece. If you just come straight down with out turning your work you will get flashing which sticks out from the sides of your work and will have to be trimmed off when done. If the material is too small it will not fill the opening of the dies and you will get an incomplete piece. As I just made the pattern from a piece of bar stock I should know what size it came from and unless I worked it down too much in making the pattern that size material should be what will work. Now the next time I use this die I may have forgotten what size material works in it so now I stamp the plate that it is mounted to with that information.

I have also used v-blocks from press brakes to make triangular bars. Not round or square stock but to make triangular bar stock. Again it is a matter of finding the right size bar to squish that matches the size of your form. In some cases round stock was better to start with and in other instances square stock was better to use. You want to match the volume of the swage opening with the volume of the bar. This is a case where you do not need a top tool, just a flat plate to push it into the tool. You should take the flap disc and round off the edges of both ends of the v-block so that you are able to work your bar down the block with out marring up your bar. It may even require a slight taper going into and out of the block so that the form will overlap and keep consistent as you work down your hot bar.

Another example of a forming or shaping die set would be used for bending door latches or pulls. If you had a large quantity of cabinet drawer pulls to do you would need to do the overall shaping in the flat first then use the dies to bend them all to the same shape. This could be done one half at a time where you would do half of the pull and then turn it around and shape the other half. You could also make tooling to do the whole pull in one push of the press.

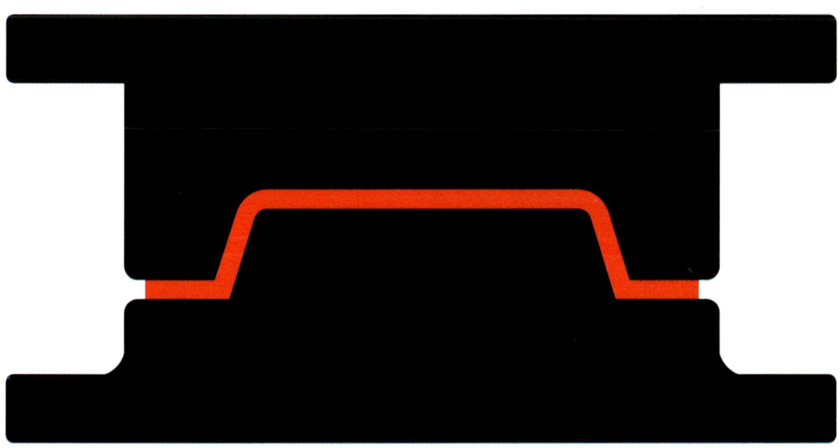

FORMING TOOLING

Forming dies for bending a handle

To make this type of tooling you need a cutout of the inside shape of the handle and a cutout of the outside shape of the handle and it needs to be at least as wide as the widest part of the handle. There would be a gap in between these for the thickness of the material used to make the handle. This could be made in a machine shop or you may be able to do it by getting the pieces water-jet cut out. Water-jet cuts at a slight angle so you would need to lightly grind both halves so they are ninety degrees from the sides. You may also be able to cut these out with a plasma or oxy/acetylene torch but then it would take a lot of cleanup to get it to the finished shape. I made one set of tooling similar to this by hot bending two heavy bars as close to the finished shape as possible and then welding in support pieces to maintain that shape under pressure.

You will also need some kind of a guide or fence to keep your work centered and straight with the tooling. If you put the work piece too far in the tooling or not deep enough your bends will be in the wrong place. It helps if your handle design has a wider area or a detail in the very center of its length. This would be a good place to put your guides so that your work piece is in the exact same location each time you do a bend. Depending on the thickness of your material and the size of your press you may be able to do this bending cold. If it does require the parts to be heated it will not require them to be forging temperature but a bright red should be enough heat.

Cut off Tool

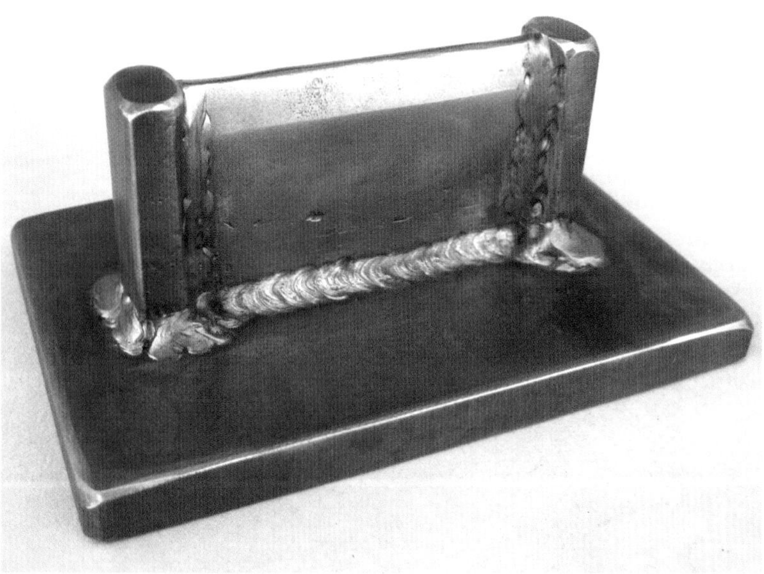

A hardie or cut off tool

A cut off tool or a long hardie is easy to make, but takes more abuse in the press than any other tool. The problem is you are pushing a big, hot piece of metal down a thin piece of metal which easily heats up and distorts. I have used leaf springs and even O-1 tool steels for this and still have had problems with the edge distorting and even folding over. I would not use mild steel for this application. Maybe the best solution is to forget making it sharp like an anvil hardie, but make a rounded edge like a very thin fuller. This would still work just as well for cutting and would hold up better in the long run.

I have seen these made from pieces of railroad rail with the rail vertical and the center web used for the cut off area and also out of "T" bar with the "T" upside down for the cut off but I have not heard how well they have held up in use. Most of the ones I have seen are made with a square post on both ends and a thinner piece of flat plate standing up in between them. I like this design because if the cutoff area is lower than the posts it provides a safety zone in that the piece can not be cut totally off which could throw your metal as it does in cutting it off on the hardie except with much more force. The end posts serve as stops for the press. This is also beneficial in making pattern welded steel. It does not cut all of the way through so creates an easy place to fold it over for your next weld without it breaking off. The pieces are just cut to length, welded together, heat treated and welded to the plate.

Dick Sexstone makes his cut offs from H13 and says that they hold up. He has a precision press and uses a top and bottom cut off. (see gallery)

It is amazing how fast this tool works. You know how in hammering a large piece of steel to cut it off on the hardie you may need more than one heat to do it? In the press I can do ten cuts in one heat! And I'm talking one inch or more square stock! This can be used for cutting off or in cutting a pattern into a bar.

Texturing Dies and Die Plates

Die plates can easily and accurately be used in a press. They can be used loose on the anvil plate or welded to a plate for quick change tooling. I use texturing or die plates loose if I only need a design pushed into one side of my work and accuracy of location is not a concern. I weld them to quick change tooling plates when I need the design from both sides of my work to hold the tooling in place or when I need an accurate top and bottom tooling alignment as in coining. Spring tooling can also be used for coining.

When I first started making die plates I had it in my mind that I needed a milling machine to cut the lines into these plates. I did not have the money or access to a milling machine and I had to figure another way to make them. Now if you do have a milling machine it will do a fine precision job of making whatever pattern that you require. CNC machines do a precision job of cutting dies of specific designs such as logos and other artwork.

Since I do a lot of die plates I get blank plates all laser cut out the same size to fit on the base plates, which were also laser cut as described earlier, with room for the guides and welding. You could cut them from a flat bar or torch them out of a steel plate.

A stack of laser cut pieces for making die plates

In not having a milling machine I decided to forge out my die plates. This can be done a couple of different ways. One way is to make up individual pieces of bar stock into a pattern and weld them together on to a larger plate so the welding does not interfere with the pattern. This could be parallel lines or wavy lines or what ever you want. This would be a positive form, or in other words it would look exactly like your finished piece that you want to forge with this die. If you pushed this into your work you would have a negative of the pattern so to make your die plate you need to push this welded piece into your die plate. Now you have a negative die plate which will produce a positive design in your finished work.

Now if you are using round stock for your positive pattern you need to be careful not to squish it into the die plate past the center of the round stock. If you do the material will get stuck in that undercut and you will not be able to remove it from the plate.

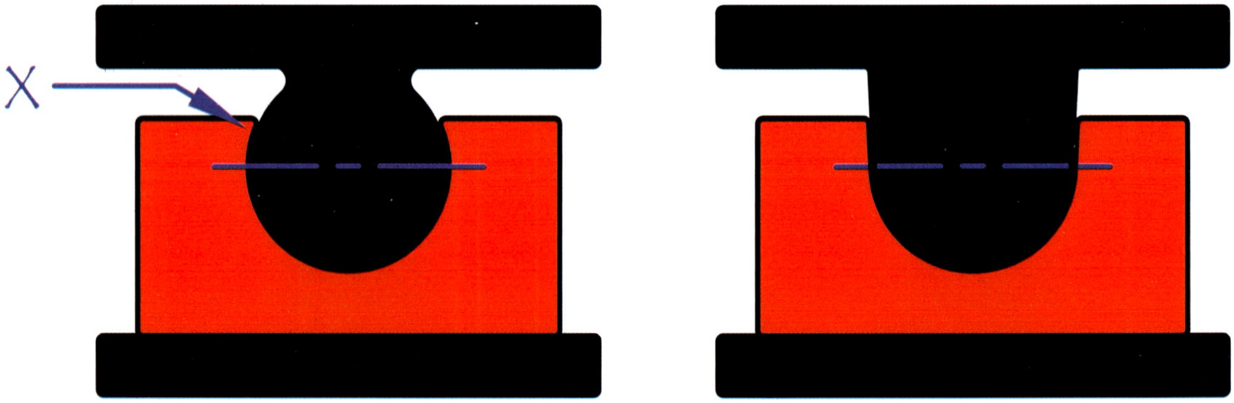

Drawing showing the problem if you push too far with an undercut piece.

If I want a curved face on my pattern lines I usually take slightly larger round stock and hammer the sides flat leaving the top and bottom rounded. In doing this you can also do the flats with angled blows so that the piece is wider at the base and thinner at the rounded top. This taper along the edge is known as draft and helps to remove the work from the pattern die. It does not take much draft in these dies to help the piece to be removed. Some of the positives I make do not have any draft to them, but pushing them into the die plate will create a slight draft on its own.

Another way to make forged die plates is to make a negative die plate without making a positive plate. This is more of a freehand design. It is done by hammering or using the press to push tooling into your die plate. In doing this you have to think backwards as anything you push into the plate will be raised out of your work. Sometimes when I am working at the press I do not want to take a lot of time making tooling to make die plates so I see what I already have handy. I have hand punches of a couple different size hearts and a star punch. I heated up my die plate and hand hammered these punches into the whole surface at the anvil. Voila, a heart and stars die plate! When the metal is pushed into this die the hearts and stars are raised up out of its surface.

The hearts and stars die plate made with hand punches on the anvil.
You can see a small plate to the right that was made using that die.

It looks like more work went into it than there was. I will say it again, do not use hand punches in the press! Only use short punches that have a handle attached to them. I will give you more information on making this tooling later.

This same process can be done with forged heads, different shaped punches, shaped bar stock or whatever you want pushed with the press into the blank die plate. I should mention that you should only use items that you know will hold up to this squishing. Do not use a commercial casting or design as it is more likely cast iron or cast brass. In using cast iron or cast brass the heat and pressure of the press could make it shatter throwing pieces at you, for some reason it never goes away from you. Maybe it is done to make a point for you not to do that?

If you want to push a head or a face into your die forge out what you want and keep in mind that you do not want any undercuts or the punch will be hard if not impossible to remove. Another nice thing about the press is that ever how much detail you put into your punch will be seen in your die and therefore in your forged work. I made a punch that was a Cheshire cats' head where I lightly carved whiskers into the face. Those whiskers are seen plainly on the finished forged piece!

The first die that I made. I pushed a forged steel Cheshire cat's head that I made into this block. To the right is a bronze head from this die. Note the amount of detail.

Coining is another process that can be done with the press using dies. Depending on the type of coin that you want to make you can use either a bottom die for a one side coin or top and bottom dies for a two sided coin. If your metal is soft enough this can be done cold, but the bronze coins that I make I do hot in order to get a deep squish with good detail. Early coins had detail on only one side and were not round but were irregular in shape. They were done on top of a die plate instead of in a die that restricts it size and shape.

The handled tooling to forge the pirate coin die with the die in the background

Pirate doubloons hot forged on the press using a die

One of the things I like about using the press for pushing in my designed tooling in making a die is that I do not have complete control of how deep they go into my die plate. So one piece goes in 1/8 of an inch the next push goes in 3/16" or whatever. This gives a more three dimensional look to your work. I have used overlapped pieces with one push deeper than the next and it has created good results. Also you don't get any echoing of the piece but one nice crisp design.

A forged bronze belt buckle that I made on the press. Here you can see the different depths of the lines made in my die using the press.

One problem with using the press to push in your punches or bars is that it is hard to see where you are putting them. As the top plate comes down it produces a shadow and blocks your view. It is just hard to see exactly where the punch is located on your die plate. This is where that shop light that I mentioned earlier can help to some degree. If you really want the location to be more precise you can start by punching the design in your die plate lightly using hammer and anvil, just enough to seat the tool when you use the press. Then use those slight depressions to locate your tooling in the press.

One of the nice things about forged die plates instead of machined die plates is that they have more life to them. There are imperfections and hammer marks and changes in thickness. So it all depends on how you want your work to look when done. There are places where the machined precision looks good and places where the forged designs look good.

If you want to see how your design is coming out while making your design in your plate, instead of heating up your material and using the press to do a trial squish, use a piece of modeling clay. The clay will work just like the hot metal and you will see how your design is working and where you may need to make any changes to your die. Make sure your die is good and cold as a warm die will melt the clay and make it difficult to remove. Clay is great for checking any of your tooling before you heat treat it and weld it to a plate. James Viste uses crumpled up aluminum foil instead of the modeling clay for the same purpose.

Keep in mind in designing a pattern for a die that the material that you are pressing into the die needs to have some where to go. As an example, if you have a plate covered with ball bearings side by side this can not push very deep into a hot piece of metal. There is no place for the hot metal to go. It would still make a nice design it just would not be as deep. If you separate the ball bearings with at least half a ball bearing gap between them you will get a deeper design. Keep in mind in this scenario not to push more than halfway on the bearing or you will not be able to remove the material.

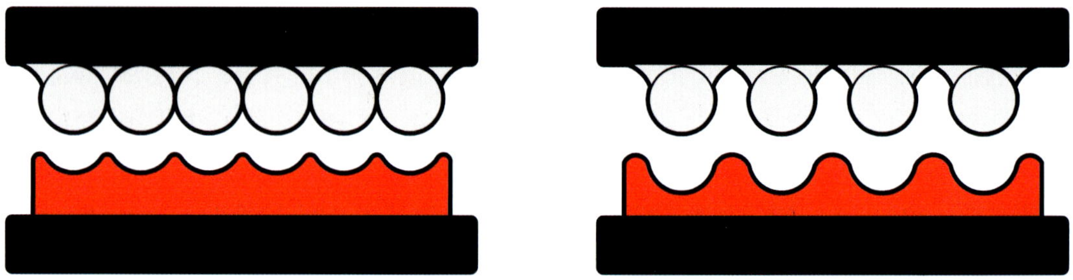

An opening is needed for material to push into for more depth.

Another way to put designs in your work is by using cnc (Computer Numeric Control) cut patterns. I like laser cutting best as it has a cleaner edge than plasma. Water-jet cutting is better cost wise for thicker material but not on thinner material. You can also use the hand held plasma cutter if the design is larger and precision is not an issue. What is also beneficial with laser cutting is how small the cutout can be and the detail it will still have. Now if you only order one part this will be fairly expensive, but if you get ten parts it will be considerably less. Either way would be less expensive than the time you would have in cutting out the design by hand and it will produce a better part.

When I get a design cut out I ask for the part and the drop. That way I get the positive and the hole that it came out of, or the negative. Now the drop will have a small hole with a lead-in line going to the edge of the cutout. This lead-in line is there so that it is not in the finished part and it gives a place for the laser to start cutting. This hole is only about 1/16 inch in diameter and the lead in line is only about 1/4 inch long and about .007 inch wide so both are very easy to weld closed and sand back to level and smooth. I take a sanding wheel or a small hand held grinding or rotary tool and slightly angle the edge of the parts so they will remove easily after squishing into the die plate. These pieces can be attached to your plate by drilling holes in them and plug welding to the plate and sanding smooth.

If you push the cold positive laser piece into the hot die plate this will produce a raised design in your work. If you push the negative or the hole that the piece came out of into the hot die plate the finished die plate will produce a recessed design in your work. As an example I used a drawing of a moose to produce a part that was only about 3/4 inch high. There is no way I could have cut out that small of a part with that much detail. It worked very well for both types of die plates.

Several laser negative and positive cutouts that I use as handled die plates showen without their handles.

Here are the results of using the laser cut die plates. Note the slot in the one disc. That is the lead in cut for the laser as this was a drop. The other disc had the same slot but was welded in before forging.

You can also use this process for cutting out patterns such as parallel lines or circles in a piece or whatever you would like. Just keep in mind that parts may fall out if not tabbed together. Here is what I mean: You can get letters cut out, either individually or as a word or sentence.

This can then be pushed into a die plate and used to put that detail into your work. Letters like "R" or "O" and the like, if not tabbed, a tab connecting the center to the letter, the center part of the letter will just fall out. So the "O" will just be an oval instead of a donut.

I have also used laser cutting to produce very detailed three dimensional dies. I wanted to make a die of a historical hand carved wooden plaque. How can I put that much detail in a steel block that is only 2-1/4 inch square? I can not carve steel the way that wood is carved and especially not with that kind of detail. I looked at the wood carving as being a mountain with high parts and low parts and thinking about that being drawn from space on a flat piece of paper. It would be a topographical map. Every thing surveyed into layers. Like taking the mountain and every fifty feet up in elevation it is horizontally cut through over and over. So I did this wood carving that way.

I ended up with four plates to be cut out. The first plate was the back or base of the carving. The next layer was what was detailed the next distance up and so on and so on with each layer until the top layer of detail. Now each of these layers had the right cutouts for where they are in the carving, but there is no surface detail to them. I used a hand held rotary tool with very small grinding bits and a lighted magnifying glass and manually cut out the curves and the detail lines in each layer. When I stacked them up in order it looked much like the original wood carving. I used small rivets to pin these layers together and then hardened the stack. This was mild steel so tempering was not required.

I welded this to a plate which then had to be pushed into another plate so that I would have the negative that was needed for the die plate. So my stack of laser parts was cold and the die plate was hot as I squished it into it. I found that care must be taken as the laser pieces are made up of thinner pieces and will heat up very fast and if they are as hot as your plate you are pushing into it will flatten out any detail in that laser cut piece. You need to push it into the plate a little bit, remove it from the plate and the press, cool it off totally and push it into the plate again repeating that process until it is at the depth that you want. I am very happy with the solution to this challenge and how it turned out.

My most detailed die to date. It was made from a stack of laser cut layers.

Flat Plates

Instead of having to remove my ram and anvil plates with the quick change tooling guides and replacing them with the flat ram and anvil plates when I want to use handled tools or in squishing metal between the flat plates I have made flat plates that slide into the quick change guides.

Flat plate to slide into the quick change tooling guides

I just used the plates that I made and hardened for my tooling and just do not weld anything to them. I do have to replace them every so often as handled tools will cut into them and the marking can go into your work. It would be a good idea to use high carbon steel to make the flat plates.

As I mentioned I have had problems with my guides being too close together and my work or handled tools will crush the guides so I made a flat plate that is wide enough to go over the opening and over both guides. I welded this to a mild steel plate with a smaller spacer plate in between that raises the larger plate above the guides. In other words there are slots down both sides of the plate where the guides can slide into. This gives me a wider area to work on and protects the guides from being damaged.

A heavy duty flat plate that is as wide as the plate

End view of the heavy duty flat plate showing the grooves for the quick change guides

Handled Tooling

As I produce a lot of handled tooling in order to make my die plates I make a number of handles in advance so all that I have to do is weld them onto the tool when needed. Most of my handles are simply 1/4 inch round stock that I have taken one end and flattened to about 1/2 to 5/8 inch long and then forge it into an open loop.

Forged handles in preparation for creating handled tooling

This open loop is made to hang over a horizontal piece of 3/8 inch round stock that is used for the hanger bar on my tool rack and gives a small handle for holding the tool.

A lot of my tooling is mild steel as I will only be using it a few times to make a die plate. If I feel I will be using it constantly or on harder metal I will use tool steel. Coil springs are a good material for this. I harden these tools in water and temper to a grey as I want it to have give in it. If you use mild steel for handled fullers the top side will probably flatten in use and eventually the bottom side will flatten and get marred up. Therefore a tool steel would be better for fullers.

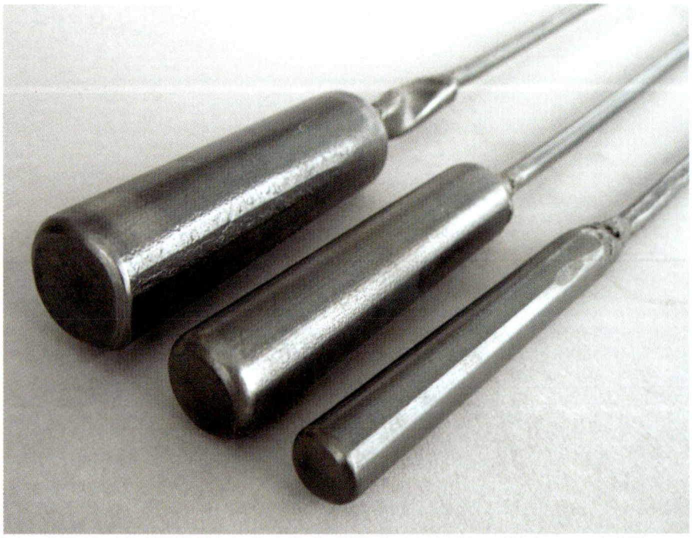

Three different sizes of handled fullers

The same is true with handled set tools. These are square stock or flat stock with a slight radius on the edges. These are used for cutting in shoulders in your work. An example of their use would be in making the shoulders for tong jaws.

Handled shouldered tooling or set tools.

Other types of handled set tools

If you are making heads, punches or chisels make sure that they are not a lot longer than they are wide. Most of these tools for the press shouldn't be any more than 2 inches long. This makes for a stronger tool with less chance of snapping in half or flipping sideways in use. I put a slight radius on the top edges to prevent it from cutting into the top plate when pushing.

A variety of handled skulls for making dies

It may be beneficial to attach the handles on heads or any item that has a top and bottom to its shape at a forty-five degree angle from the tool. This way the handle is not blocking your sight when using the tool. A touch mark or signature stamp is a good example of this. The handle at a forty-five makes it easy to see exactly where you are placing it on your work.

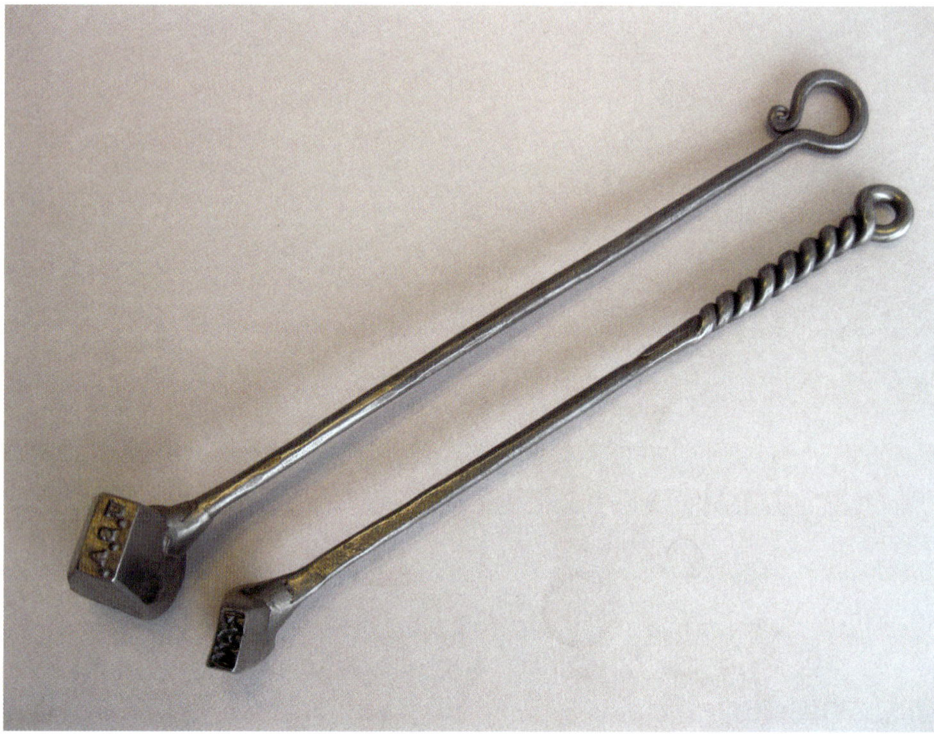

Handled touchmarks. The handles are attached at a 45 degree.
These sit on my forge not on the handled tool rack.

Tooling Racks and Die Plate Racks

Now that you have all of your tooling…no, that is not usually how that works… you will probably start with a few basic tools and the more you use your press the more tooling you will want and you will find new ways of using it. The problem soon becomes that you have piles of tooling and the quick change tooling becomes "quick" only if you can find the tools. So some sort of tool display system becomes imperative. I say "display" as you need to see your tooling not just put it in a rack.

The goal was to have a way that with one quick glance I could see the tool I want, grab it and install it in the press. Once I'm ready for the next tool the first one goes back in place and I can grab the next tool that is needed. I settled on an A-frame stand for my anvil and ram plates and for my quick change tooling. I also need a separate rack for all of my die plates and for my handled tooling.

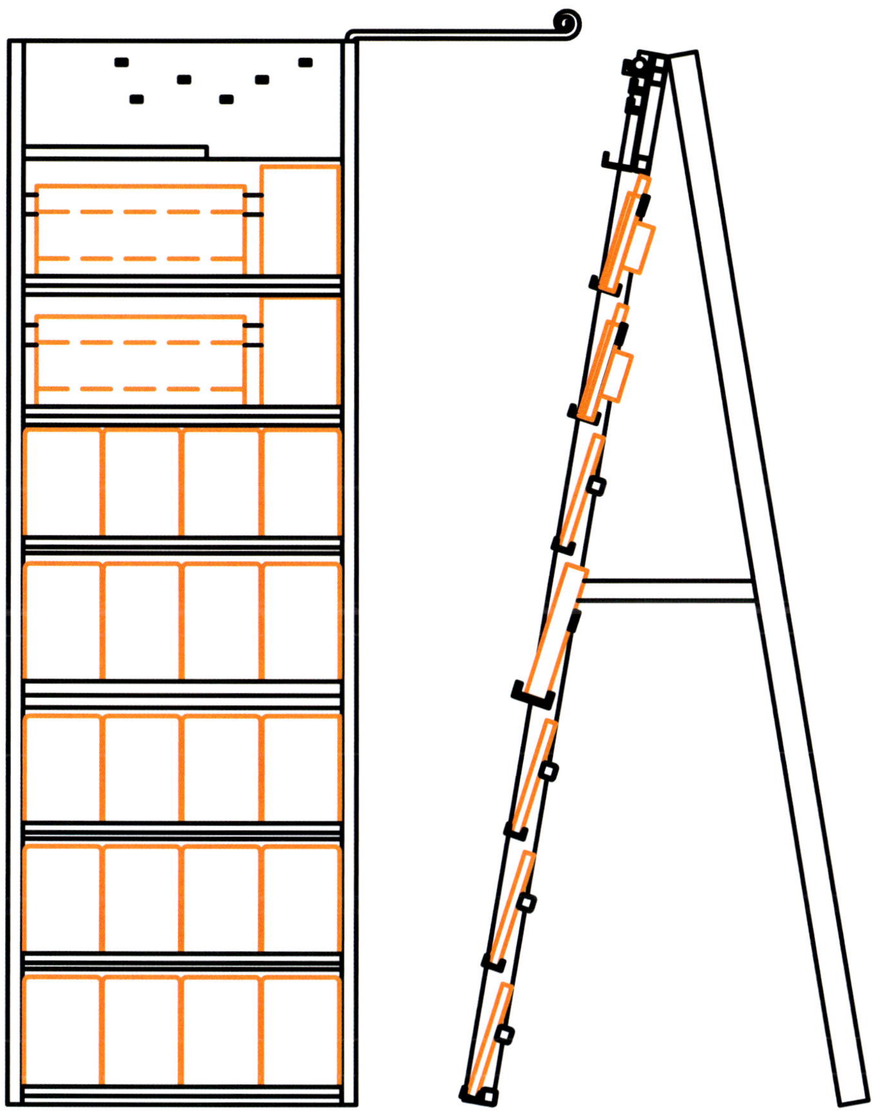

A-FRAME TOOL RACK

The A-frame rack was easy to make, is sturdy and works very well. It helps if you plan ahead with your design in figuring what you will be putting on the rack and where you want the different tools. I have the flat anvil and ram plates, but I also have the same size plates with my quick change tooling set up on it. This meant that I needed some where for two large plates. The balance of the tooling is for the quick change tooling and they all have the same size back plates so this made spacing easy.

A lot of the tooling is top heavy as it sticks out from the plate so this tooling has to lean back in order not to fall off of the rack. The angle of the A-frame helps in this, but more of an angle is still required. I used 1-1/2 inch channel to hold the bottom of the tooling and a support strap or bar about 4 inch up from the channel. The channel is welded on the front of the frame and the back support is welded on the back of the frame. This allows the tooling to lean back more and provides less chance of falling off of the rack. My top two rows are for the flat plates and the remainder is for five rows of quick change tooling. This rack gives me spacing for twenty top or bottom tools. I also have a space on the very top area for tooling that is used for loosening and tightening bolts and extra bolts right there in case any break.

Even placement of your tools on the rack is helpful in locating what you need to use next. What ever tooling you use most put on the top row and work down from there. I have my top and bottom fuller/flatter combo first then I group punches on the next row, fullers on the next row and odd tooling below that. That is just what works for how I use the press. Your arrangement could be totally different.

Now I have the stripper plate and guide system for punching holes, which is the same size as the anvil and ram plates, so I do not have any where to put it on the rack. Plus I have the top and bottom bowl tooling, well, you get the idea. I need another rack!

I used tubing for my A-frame as I had it on hand. I got tired of going through a pile of handled tooling to find what I needed so decided to add a horizontal bar to my A-frame for this purpose. I welded a plate across the top opening of the tubing that had a slightly oversized 3/8 inch diameter hole in the center. I forged a closed up scroll on one end of a 3/8 inch round bar and bent the other end at a ninety degree angle. That end fits in the hole in the top plate which supports this horizontal bar. It also swivels if I need to pull it towards me or push it out of the way. The loops on my handles tools have a gap that is slightly larger than 3/8 inch so that I can hang the tools over the bar. This has worked very well for me. I've already added another bar on the other side of the rack for more tooling. Both racks are already full!

Handled tooling on the horizontal rack

You could use the horizontal cross member of your A-frame to hang your tongs in order to get them closer to your press and not mixed up with your other forging tongs. I had to weld tie down bars onto my press in order to transport it for demonstrations and classes and I use one of those for my tong rack.

Tong rack on the side of the press

It may be a bit harder to develop a rack for your die tooling, especially one that allows you to see some part of each design in order to find the die that you need. Even though these are not top heavy like the other tooling they are still heavy and need to lean back so they do not fall out of the rack if you stand them on edge. I am still looking for a better solution for this rack design as I currently have over sixty-five die plates. Some smiths use a tool cabinet with drawers and lay the plates flat in the drawers. This is good for viewing their designs, but due to the size of the plates they take up a lot of space. These cabinet drawers are different depths and a 4 inch deep drawer can only hold the same number of dies as a 1 inch deep drawer. I was thinking about making a drawer type system but with flat boards or plate that would slide in and out. That way I could space them about 2 inches apart and cut down on the height of the overall unit.

Currently I have a rack that I welded up from 3/8 inch round stock. This sits on a table next to the A-frame rack. It is an open grid of bars that allows the dies to stand up and lean back so they don't fall over. This does a good job of separating the plates and allows grouping of designs.

Overflowing die rack on a separate table

The problem is that they are all the same height so I can not see what is behind the one in front of it and so I have to "flip" through each one to find what I want. It is better than a pile of them but it still needs improvement. Maybe I could try a similar design but with each row being stepped higher than the row before it. Then each row would have to have a bottom in it where now the table top serves as the bottom for all of them. We keep growing and learning as we live and work.

Tooling for Pattern Welded Steel

This includes the previously shown fuller and flatter combination for drawing out and flattening your billet and the cut off tool to cut the billet for folding it over for the next weld. Squaring tools need to be top and bottom tooling and can be made up of heavy wall angle iron or use a v-block in the press and make your own solid triangular pieces to weld up for this tool. Or have a big block and push a triangular bar into it to forge out the forms that are needed.

SQUARING TOOLS

FRONT VIEW

Pattern dies for pattern welded steel. These should come under the heading of die plates as they are used to squish a pattern into the stack of material to produce a design in the layers. These are usually very precise designs with equal spacing in the design. You could fabricate a ladder die by laying side by side material of the width and depth that you want in your tooling. Then weld every other piece down to the plate and then remove the pieces in between. This could be used as is or it could be pushed into another die block to create the same design. If you really want it to be precise then cut out your patterns using a milling machine.

LADDER TOOLS

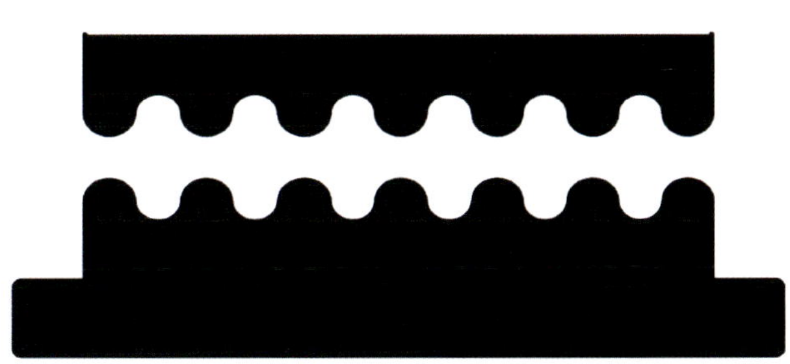

END VIEW

Some pattern dies for this application are simply a plate that has been randomly electric welded all over the surface to create a texture. If you make two plates like this you can push the pattern into both sides of your billet at once. It doesn't work to use one die plate as it will only do one side and when you turn your piece over to do the other side the press will flatten out your first pattern.

Other configurations can also be used simply by applying information previously shown.

11 Personal Gallery of More Press Tooling

Another type of punch holder. I had problems with this design as the punch would pull out of the holder when retracting the punch from the hole.

A handled ball swage to be used on the top or bottom of your work to round it off.

Handled scrolls of various sizes to squish into hot metal.

A couple of paper weights made with the scroll tooling.

Handled squiggly tooling to use directly into the finished piece or to make dies.

Handled snail tooling to make dies to produce 3-D snails.

Hand punch used to make the diamond plate die with a piece of bronze used to make the diamond plate belt buckle.

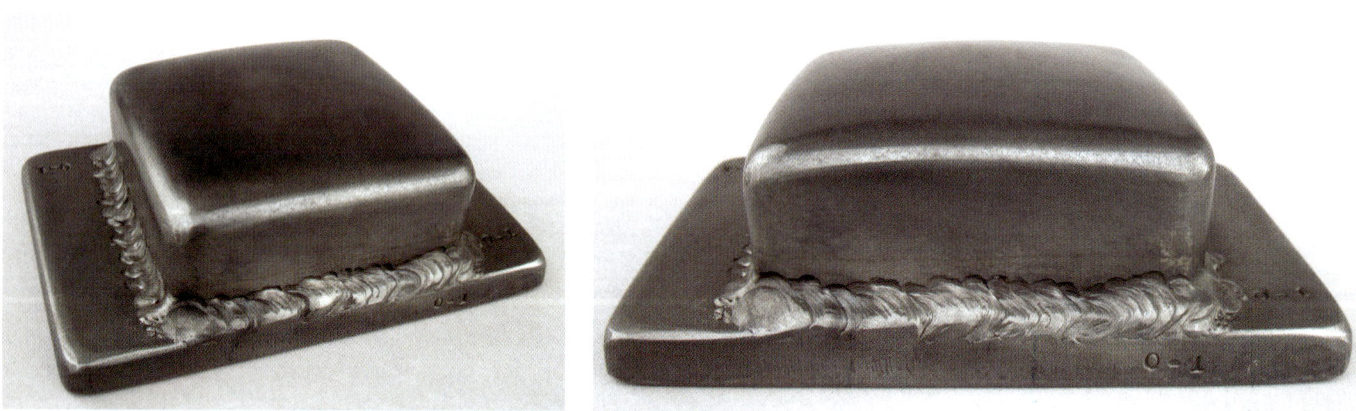

This is a top tool. It is good for forging larger material as the shape of its face is slightly domed and therefore gets more force at the center and less as it works outward from the center. It helps to lessen the pounds per square inch problem by centering the force in a smaller area.

I thought I would show the set up on my H-frame press. Here you can see the center plate and the two outer plates which make up my ram guides and give me a recess for mounting my ram plate or ram plate with quick change tooling guides.

This is my ram plate viewed from the bottom. You can see how this fits into the ram plates in the previous photo with holes to accept the mounting bolts.

The bottom ram plate with quick change tooling guides installed in the ram plates. There are stops welded into the ends of both angles to prevent the tooling from sliding out of the back.

Now shown with a piece of half inch square bar slid up to the stops.

Here is the set up being used with the combo fuller and flatter tooling on the bottom and flat plate on the top.

I forged this hand life size to use as a tool for pushing my hand into hot steel! Due to its size it takes many heats to push the whole tool into a plate using a sixty ton press.

Handled tooling made to create positive or negative anvils and sabers. The positive tools were made for making negative dies.

12 Operation of the Hydraulic Forging Press

By now you have a pretty good idea of what a forging press can accomplish, its tooling and its basic operation. I want to go over the process of actually using the press for forging.

If you have used a power hammer a lot of this will sound familiar, but I would rather cover this process than let it go to chance. If you have not used a power hammer before this information will be good for using that, too.

As in any forging operation it is important to think and plan ahead. It is important to figure out what you are going to do before you do it. Know what steps are required to achieve the finished results. Then you can get the material and the tooling needed to accomplish those tasks. That includes your tongs and the press tooling. This will also be a time saver. It can be frustrating to be in the middle of a forging operation and then realize that you need a specific tool and then either you can not find it or you have to stop and make it.

Before starting inspect the press frame, attachment bolts and hoses for any problems. Check the floor near your press for any signs of oil leakage. Fix any problems before going to the next step.

Once this is done you can do a cold run of the operation you plan on doing. Leave the fire and the press off, install the first tooling in the press that you will need and do a walk through. That means stand where your fire will be, take your material in your hand or in your tongs and then turn and walk to the press and put the material on the lower tooling. How did that go? Was there something in the way that you need to move? Was there something on the floor in the way? Move it now. Were you able to reach the tooling with your material all the way through the press with out getting your hand in there? If not you need a longer piece of material so stop and cut a new piece. If your next step involves turning the work piece in another direction will the same tongs still work or do you need another pair of tongs? Get them now.

Turn on the press and start to close the plates just to a point where your material can fit easily in between the plates or tooling. Now turn the press off. Is anything in the way of the tooling closing? Does your tooling line up? Can you move your material in what ever way it has to be moved without restriction such as hitting your tooling guides? Figure out the solutions to any problems before you start to forge.

I know this may sound like a lot of preparation but it only takes five or ten minutes in the beginning of your job if you already have the tongs and tooling that you need and it will save you time and save you from possible dangerous safety issues in the long run.

Turn on the press and make sure it can go the full distance up and down with out any problem. If it is cold in your shop you should let the press run for about ten minutes to heat up the hydraulic oil. Then operate the press up and down several times. If you don't do this the cold oil flow will be restricted and you will not get your full power to your work. The press will stall instead of squish. This can even cause the motor to strain and may even blow your circuit breaker.

If you have every thing ready to go then you are ready to hot forge. Close your press with just enough room to put your metal in the opening. Why would you want to heat up your work, bring it to the press and wait for the jaws to close on your work? Save time and save heat by having the opening so that you start squishing right away. When you squish to the depth that you want open the tooling just enough so that you can move or turn your work for the next squish, not the whole distance of the opening. Now repeat this until that operation is done or your work is too cold to work any more.

If your tooling is cold when you start forging it will not be cold for long. Initially the cold tooling will pull heat from your material but soon that will be lessened as the tooling heats up. The size of your material affects this, too. I have squished some stock where you can see the heat color brighten as the forging is done. The friction of the squishing action actually heats up your material. Small material won't have as long of a time in the press because it has gotten too cold, but you will see how much more work was accomplished compared to hand hammering.

You learn each time you use the press. How far to push before moving the piece or turning the piece before the next squish comes with experience. If you are trying to figure out how to create something for the first time use a piece of modeling clay and squish it in between your fingers. The result will be the same with hot metal in the press. Your fingers would be top and bottom fullers.

Similar to using a power hammer it is important to keep your bar stock horizontal in the press. In using a power hammer if you have the metal at an angle instead of straight in the dies it can throw the bar up at you. You do not have this same problem in the press as the energy of the press is not a quick hit but a slower squish into the metal. The metal will rise up but not like the swinging of a bat. Not having your work level will cause your tooling not to line up when it squishes your work. The top tool will hit slightly down the bar from the bottom tool if you are leaning down on your work and the opposite condition if you raise the bar higher than level.

There may be times that your work piece may need some adjustment that you can not fix with the power of the press unless you take the time to change tooling. Here the hammer and anvil may work best. Some times the power and speed of the press has done more than you wanted it to do and now your work is bent in a way that you do not want. Heat the piece and strike it with the hammer on the anvil to straighten the bend. Then you can take another heat and again work in the press. Minor adjustments like this may be a normal process in press work.

If you are upsetting a piece in the press vertically the piece should be as straight up and down as possible. If your work is at an angle to the anvil and ram plates your work will push those plates in the direction of the angle. As long as the work piece is good and hot most of the energy will go into the work, but some will still go into the tooling and plates. This could be a dangerous situation. I usually hold a piece that I am upsetting with tongs until it gets so low that the tongs are in the way.

As the piece is being upset it will start swelling in the middle so you will have to start opening your tongs so it will not interfere with this. Once you feel the work piece will not move you can let go of it and keep squishing. Plus once the work is squished to a point where it is wider than it is tall the energy is going down instead of sideways and there is little chance of the piece sliding or pushing the tooling.

The process of vertical upsetting

I find it interesting, too, that putting a texture or design on the side of your piece before upsetting will distort that pattern or design into a unique design or pattern. Also if you have a dramatic upset you can see the size of the original bar and sometimes even the texture on the side of that bar on the bottom of the finished upset.

The texture pushed into the sides of this piece distorted into a snake skin design when upset. Note the outline of the original size bar on the bottom.

If you want more swelling in the upsetting at the top than in the middle or bottom of your bar, cool off those areas before you start upsetting. Do not do this with tool steels as the cooling will harden it and it could break when pressing. Localized quenching can be a handy technique in press work if done carefully.

Depending on the tooling and how your squishing turned out you may need to straighten or true up your work before returning to the press. Simply heat the work and hammer it on your anvil to what is required.

Back to your work in progress: If you just need to reheat your work then do that and continue working. If you have finished that step in your forging and you need other tooling remove the current tooling with the handle if it has one or with tongs or locking pliers. This tooling is very hot from constant contact with the hot metal. You may want to quickly dip this tooling in and out of your slack tub and then let the tool steam off the water while it sits on the floor or a metal table where you are not likely to grab it again. The dipping in water will just prevent the tool from getting too hot and lose its temper. Do not cool the tool all of the way to cold as it could crack the tool depending on what type of steel was used in its construction. Plus if you will be using that tool again it is already preheated. Just remember not to pick it up with your hands.

You will continue like this until your work is finished. Once done I open the rams and anvil plates so that the cylinder shaft is fully in the cylinder. This will protect the shaft from dirt, moisture and rust.

As mentioned before the front apron helps to keep dirt and scale away from the cylinder and shaft for a lower cylinder press. My front apron was made from stainless steel sheet and is sturdy. I find this front apron handy for holding handled tooling in preparation for when I need it.

I also use an adjustable work table/cart, similar to an auto mechanic's tool cart without drawers. It has a small tray on top that can be raised up or down and casters for moving it where you want. Mine came with a plastic tray so I would recommend replacing it with a steel tray. I did find one such cart that had a two hundred pound capacity with an all steel construction and was about fifty dollars. This is handy for your tooling at the press and it can be lowered for tooling when working at the anvil.

An auto mechanics' tool cart used to hold tooling at the press

It is also convenient to have a five gallon bucket of water near your press for cooling off your tooling. Make sure it is a metal bucket as you could melt a hole in the bottom or lower side of a plastic bucket if you accidentally drop your hot piece in the water due to the size of your tooling.

Once you are finished using the press run the ram plate until the cylinder rod is totally encased in the cylinder. This will protect the rod from rust or any other damage. Then turn off the electric switch. There is a good chance of your tooling or dies rusting as you had to quench them due to the heat that was absorbed in use. You may want to take some time to wire wheel any tooling used in the press and cover with some type of penetrating oil or rust inhibitor before placing them back in the tool rack.

I should also mention that limit switches can add another dimension to your work capabilities. The ability to control how far you are pushing the tooling and how far you are raising it to start the next push gives the ability to do other operations that would be difficult to do with out the use of limit switches. This would allow you to do work similar to what is done using a fly press such as pushing into cold metal in order to create lines and designs by pushing to a specified depth repeatedly. You could also work sheet metal cold for free forming of bowls. Here is a good place where working aluminum cold would not be a problem. Keep your mind open for other uses of the press.

Inlaying

Another process that you can do with the press is inlaying. I had some small, 1-3/8 inch long, brass dragonflies laser cut out for a sign I was making. I heated up a square bar of steel and upset it to give the sides character. Then while it was still hot I placed one of the cold dragonflies on top and squished again. Probably if I would keep digging and prying at it I might be able to get it out, but it is pretty secure. It would be fun to try a similar process with inlaying cold brass or copper wire into a piece of steel. Keep in mind if the copper or brass gets hot it will deform before pushing into the hot steel.

A laser cut brass dragonfly inlayed into a steel block with the press

Stacking

Another process is stacking. I wanted to make some money using the press so decided I would try making a dollar sign in steel. I forged out the "S" and then prepared two straight pieces for the uprights. While all pieces were hot I laid down the "S" on the flat plate, positioned the two uprights and squished down with the other flat plate. These pieces will not come apart!

A pressed dollar sign with a texture die and results

This photo also shows a texturing die and the results of using it on a piece of hot bronze.

I had a bunch of scrap cutoffs, heated them, quickly piled them up in the press and squished. These will not come apart. You may get one or two pieces at first that will fall off, but the rest are there to stay. You can see in the photo that the pieces form around each other to hold them in place.

A stack of scrap, or a scrap pile.

You may want to experiment using this technique in creating other assemblies or unions, either as a group of pieces or as a union for a corner or just two parts coming together.

Gas Forge

I should also add that one of the things that has helped my press work is the gas forge that I use. My background has been using the coal forge, but for press work the gas forge does a great job. I get a thorough fast heat with lower scale than many of the other gas forges. Plus it is a lot hotter than most other atmospheric gas forges.

My gas forge with the Steve Gensheimer burner and air curtain.

The one that I am using the most has an atmospheric burner built by Steve Gensheimer. Steve also builds and sells complete forges using the same burner. This burner combined with an insulated freon tank has produced a very hot, lower scale, compact and economical forge. It is economical not only in the cost of the forge, but also in the amount of gas that it burns. I can even forge weld with it. My previous gas forges did not compare to the heat that I can get with this forge.

I like the way it is lit, too. Instead of putting on the gas and throwing something burning into the forge opening and it exploding as it lights all of the gas at once, with this burner you simply adjust your tank pressure to about 5 pounds pressure and put a match at one of the burner vent holes. This lights the gas as it goes through the burner instead of in the forge chamber. Smart!

The upper hinged door on the front produces a hotter heat by keeping more heat in the forge as it doesn't allow the upper heat to escape. I was surprised at how much hotter the forge became just by adding that half door.

I also added an air curtain on the front of the forge. I had heard of these but never understood how this could be beneficial. Usually the simple things are the best. I used an old blower hooked up with a metal flex hose like those used for clothes dryer vents and it just blows straight up. This takes the dragon's breath that is blowing right at you and blows it up and away from you taking the heat with it. It also helps to stop the heat from traveling up the bar that you are heating in the forge. I have had a lot of students that have used gas forges use this one and they are surprised at how well a simple idea like this works.

This forge sits on a metal table with casters so that I can move it to where ever it is convenient to use. I drilled holes in the table sides, welded short pieces of pipe behind the holes and my tool/metal rests just slide in and out to what ever distance I need to support my metal while heating.

13 Forging Pipe and Tubing

Some say to not use pipe in forging as the seam will split open. That can be true in some poor quality pipe and pipe that has rusted, but I have done a lot of pipe forging with no problem at all. It would be good to keep in mind that it could split so work it good and hot and keep an eye out for any problems.

Tubing or seamless pipe can be forged into a lot of different shapes and designs. One interesting design is to cut a piece of pipe/tubing short enough to stand upright in the flat plates of your press and just squish. This will be a pretty much a free form squish in that you do not have any control as to where any folding of the material goes. One way to get some control is to heat the pipe with an oxy/acetylene torch where you want it to fold and leave the rest of the pipe cold. You can also heat up your pipe and use a fuller on opposite sides of your pipe and start pushing in the sides. Move the location and do it until you have your piece marked for the design that you want to create. Then heat up the whole pipe, place it in the press vertically and squish. The pipe will buckle in at each one of your fuller marks. Your design will change depending on how far you squish the pipe. Some times it looks better with a little squish, other times with a deep squish. This design can be used for bowls, candle holders, parts for grille work or where ever you see fit.

Small dish made by upsetting pipe.

Be very careful in cooling pipe as placing a hot piece of pipe in water will produce a hot stream of steam flying out the end of the pipe and that end is usually aimed towards you. Closing the non working end of the pipe with a wooden plug or wet rag will prevent that steam spray and will also help to stop the heat from traveling up the pipe. Still be careful that in quenching the end of the pipe that steam doesn't blow the plug out of the end you are holding.

Any other forging operations using pipe/tubing is done exactly the same way as it is with hammer and anvil or on the power hammer using the same tooling fitted to the press. The difference is in the source of power.

14 Cold Work for Sheet Metal

Not all work in a press is done hot. Depending on the size of material and the tonnage of your press cold bending can be done. Besides using the previous bending tools you can use tooling that is similar to that used in a press brake which has sharper wedges coming in from the top and "V" swages as your bottom tool. As mentioned before some forming tooling for bending handles can also be done cold.

Jewelers use a bench top bottle jack press for cold forming softer non-ferrous metals such as copper, brass, bronze, gold and sliver. These are usually a 20 ton press and they operate by hand instead of a motor and run much slower than a forging press.

Potter USA 20 ton bottle jack press (© KPotter)

Some jewelers do use an air assisted bottle jack press. They use the press for folding, cutting out shapes, embossing, inlaying and shaping sheet metal and smaller pieces of material. There is also tooling for shaping bracelets, coining and other operations.

Maybe some of these processes can be of benefit to you?

In order to cut out repeated shapes faster in sheet metal jewelers use what is known as pancake or shearing dies and blanking dies.

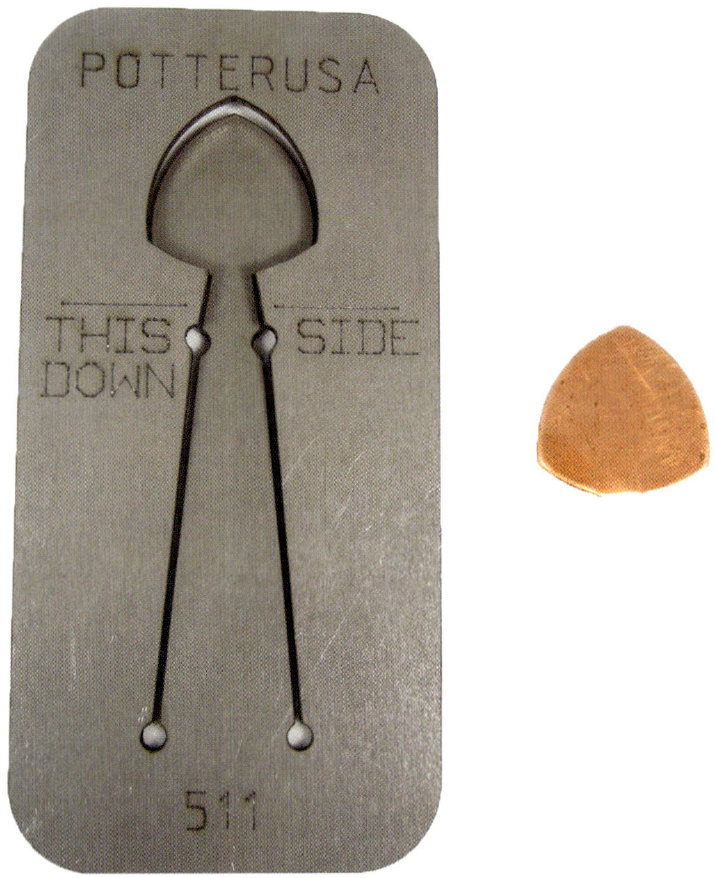

Pancake die sprung open and the sample of the cutting next to it. The little extra piece at the bottom of the metal already trimmed off. (© KPotter)

These are usually set up for material that is 20 gauge to 1/16 inch thick. Pancake dies can be heat treated tool steel sheet that has a line cut in it of the required shape to be cut out with longer lines extending past it to provide a spring action and spacing to slide your metal to be cut into. The design for the cut out can be as simple as a circle to an elaborate leaf or other detailed outline. To use a pancake die the metal that you want to cut out is placed in the die by springing the die open and sliding in the metal. Then put this in the press and close the press until you hear the metal "pop". You will have one small area to clean up but is saves a lot of time in sawing. They are very economical, too. They run around $20.00 each and will last for hundreds of cuttings.

You can also use a silhouette die along with a piece of urethane in order to__ emboss your metal.

A silhouette die (© KPotter)

Urethane is a soft plastic that you can push metal into and it will return to its shape when done using it. The softness or hardness of urethane is measured in various durometers. Silhouette or embossing dies are used to put a design or pattern into the surface of the material. These are used with a design that has already been cut out. Place your metal on top of the urethane, the die on top of that and then close the press to the depth that you want to make your design. To get a deeper embossed design, use a steel container with the piece of urethane and then a metal pusher on top. The container helps to get a deeper draw in your design.

Steel container for urethane and two steel pushers. (© KPotter)

You can also use the press for forming the sheet metal shape as in making half of an acorn in sheet metal. A forming die is a plate with the shape that you want to form cut out in it. A piece of urethane is put down first then your forming die on top of that. Then place your metal in or on the die with another piece of urethane on top of that and close the press. The top piece of urethane will push down to form the inside of the acorn and the lower piece of urethane will support the outside shape.

A silhouette die used as a forming die for making domed shapes. (© KPotter)

You can also use top and bottom embossing dies for whatever shape that you want to achieve. These dies can be purchased from jewelry supply stores for standard forms or you can make them yourself. Liz Wallace makes her dies by using liquid steel.

Homemade top and bottom press dies by Liz Wallace (©LWallace)

Liquid steel is an epoxy resin with a large amount of steel powder in it. Some are made for making molds and they can be machined and have a high compressive strength. As with most epoxies there are safety issues to learn with each type and formula. They can be very dangerous in the liquid state and safety glasses and nitrile gloves must be worn. Read all of the descriptions and warnings that come with which ever brand and formula you have chosen to use.

Liz made hers by sculpting the desired finished form out of clay for the positive form, setting a piece of pipe over it and then pouring in the liquid steel. She then uses the same process to make the negative die form. Keep in mind that there should be spacing in between these two dies of the thickness of the material that you plan to shape.

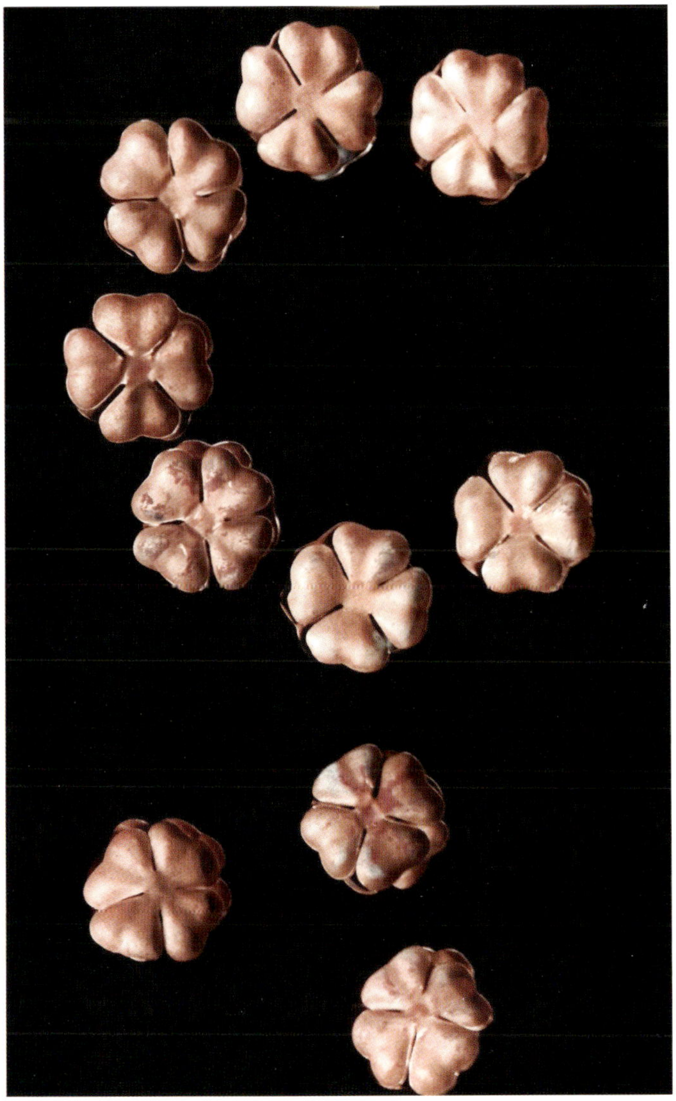

Copper flowers made using dies in the press (©LWallace)

Jewelry made by Liz from the flowers (©LWallace)

I must point out that this is for cold work only! The so called high temperature mold maker epoxies can only withstand 500 degrees Fahrenheit. So far I have not found any liquid steel or any liquid metal epoxy that goes higher than that. Also check what compression it will withstand so as not to crush it in the size press that you are using. Even with this restriction it still can be a useful tool in die making for cold pressing of softer non ferrous metals.

Another material that may be considered for cold work is deep draw steel sheet. This material is also known as AK steel which stands for "aluminum killed" steel and may be listed as 1008 Aluminum Killed Drawing Quality steel. Formally it is listed as ASTM A1008 DS Type B. The nice thing about this steel is that it is worked cold and is about 20% to 30% softer than regular 1018 mild steel sheet and stretches to a greater depth than other steels. Due to this it is used extensively in the automobile manufacture and other industry. Even metal fabrication shops that specialize in automobile restoration or custom hot rods and motorcycles also use this material to form fenders, gas tanks and other sheet metal parts.

It is fairly easy to purchase this steel across the country once you know the above specification, but many of these suppliers have minimum orders of $200 or more. One supplier's minimum was 3,000 pounds. You also have to buy in full 4' x 8' or larger sheets. Pricing was not much different than cold rolled steel sheets of the same thickness.

So the advantage of this deep draw steel is that you can form it cold. If you are going to heat it you won't gain any benefit over regular mild steel sheet worked hot. This material may be a solution to the liquid steel dies not withstanding heat if you need steel instead of copper, brass or precious metal. It will also speed up production as you are not waiting for it to heat up or handling hot material and you still can get a deep push to your design.

These are just simple descriptions of these processes and if you are interested in learning more about this I recommend you take some jewelry classes where presses are used. This is becoming even more popular in recent years due to some less expensive bottle jack presses being available and craft schools and press makers are carrying more courses in its use.

This has been just some of the tooling and ways that the press can be used. The gallery will give you other ideas and show you some fine work that was done on the press. Hopefully this will open your mind to the versatility of the hydraulic forging press in your shop. Have fun with it and keep safety in mind at all times.

15 Gallery of Press Work By Randy McDaniel

My Earliest Press work

My first pressed piece using a bottom fuller, a texturing die and the ram and anvil plate. I wanted the upper portion to look like it was squeezed in my hand with the hot metal squishing between my fingers.

Experimental pieces using the top and bottom fuller/flatter combo and top and bottom fuller.

Playing with pushing a scroll into upset pieces and inlaying. The lower left and right pieces are upset titanium.

Tire On A Tire

A wrought iron wagon tire with a tire track running through it.

A wrought iron bowl. Squished to show the grain of the material.

A steel and a wrought iron candle holder. Both textured before squishing and punching.

A box made of pure iron. The lid is pushed on with it hot and the box cold for a perfect fit.

A bowl made of layers of steel forge welded, drawn out, and shaped, all done in the press.

Just some of the forged bronze belt buckles I have made using my forged dies in my press.

Column of Spirits
Cane or walking stick handle. Solid hot forged bronze.

I have been told so many times to keep my fingers out of the press... Life size, hot forged bronze.

16 Gallery of Presses, Metalwork and Tooling

Here you will see other press ideas, press tooling and other ways of working.

Antonio Diaz Garcia
Spain

Rigor | 2011
cm 120x30x27
Massive iron

Reverses | 2010
cm 120x50x50
Massive iron

Recogimiento | 2009
cm 132x35x19
Stainless steel

Joshua Goss
Denver, Colorado

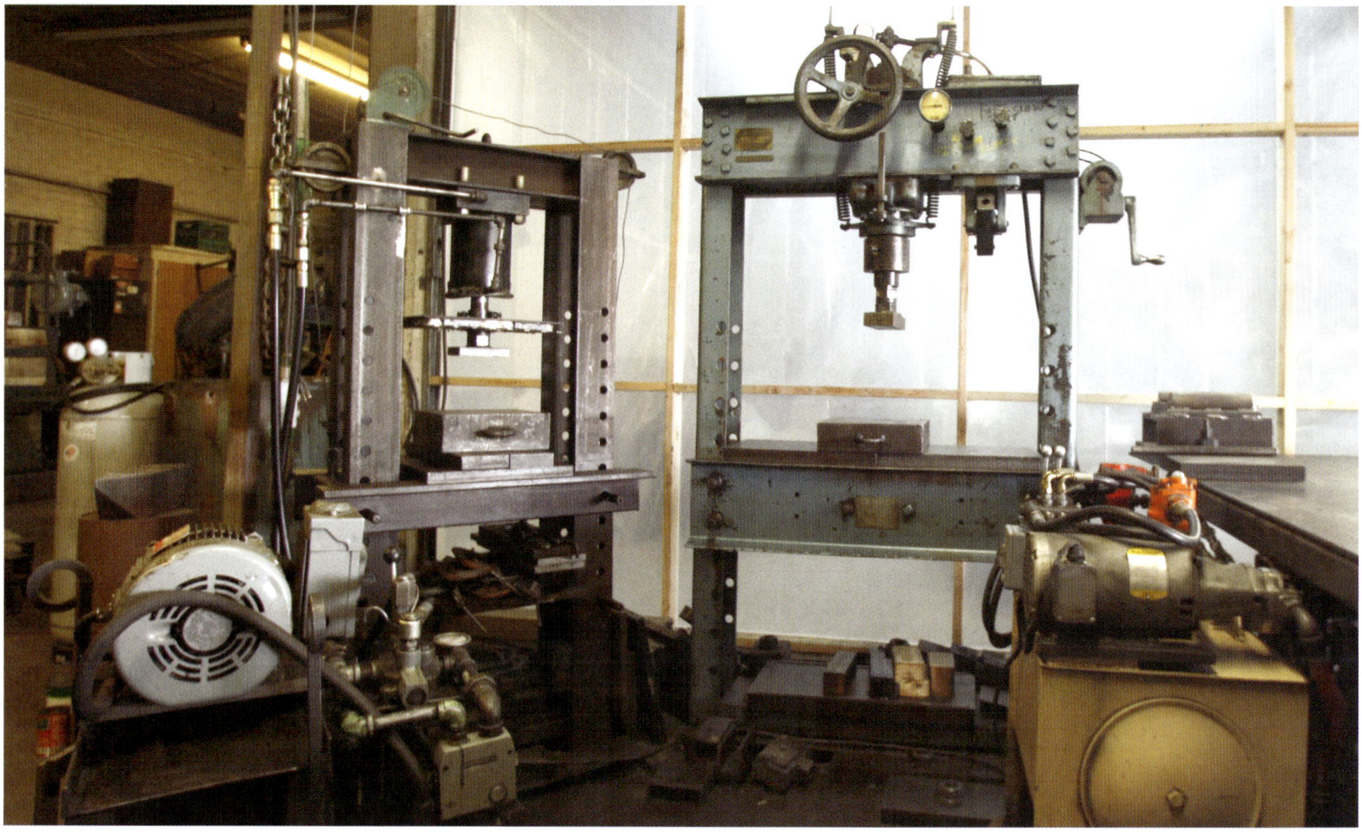

"I do not have a pneumatic forging hammer. I use these presses for the majority of forging operations in my shop."

Joshua has two industrial shop presses. A single acting, 60 ton on the right and a 18 tons, double acting press. Both have external power packs.

Forge welding, fullering and manipulating stacks of forge welded iron and steel in his press for his recent sculptures.

Joshua Goss
Denver, Colorado

"I make sculpture using metal fabrication and blacksmithing techniques that stimulate geological processes and transformations."

These are some of his current body of work just completed, called *Ductile Compression*.

The red is inlayed plastic.

Nebojsa Ilijevic
Belgrade, Šebia

Nebojsa built this 20 ton press himself using information he found on the internet.

Due to the different work that he does his anvil height can be changed by installing different lengths of heavy wall pipe. If he had a piece of solid round bar welded at the bottom to slide the pipe over it would be sturdier and safer.

As you can see he also has a tire hammer.

Yes, he has times when he uses it for a log splitter. You can see some of his bending plates to the left.

Nebojsa Ilijevic
Belgrade, Sebia

Nebojsa built this forming tooling for his press. He bends 1/2" and 1" round steel bar with it.

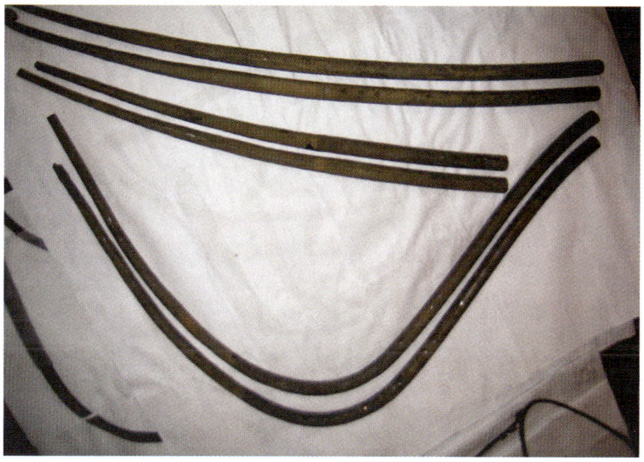

He says he has bent between 600-700 bars!

You can see he has gotten a lot of use out of it!

Bruce Jarrell
Severna Park MD

Bruce's press is about 4' to 5' tall and is rated at about 75 to 80 tons. It is an example of an industrial press. It came out of a jewelry company.

Handled ring tooling for the Ceremonial Mace.

Handled Tooling

Bruce Jarrell
Severna Park MD

Ceremonial Mace

Created for the School of Nursing at the University of Maryland.

Even the detail in the cross was done using the press.

An extraordinary job of die making.

The positive on the right was pushed into the hot die plate on the left to produce the three dimensional serpent and chalise.

The balance of the design was done by chasing by hand.

Bruce Jarrell
Severna Park MD

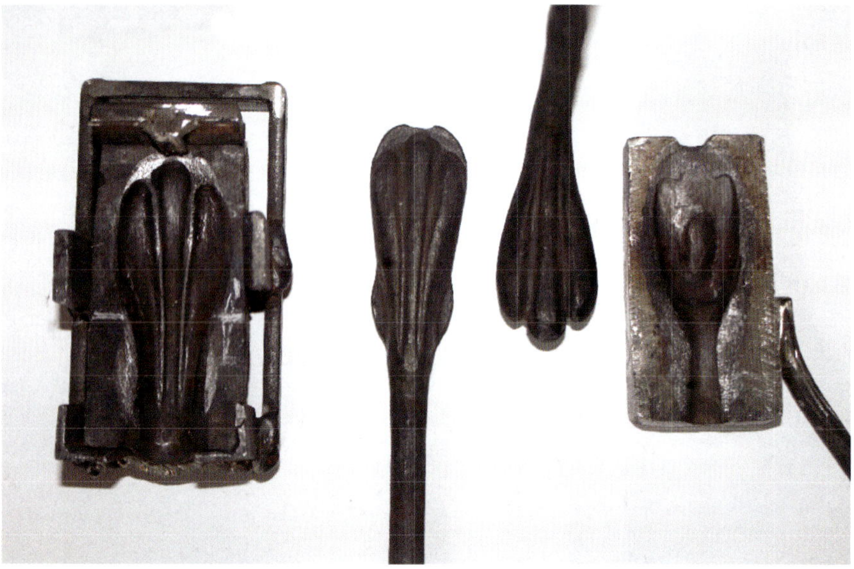

Forging feet dies to make feet for furniture in the press.

This is a top and bottom die made by pushing a finished foot into the hot metal.

Either upset the end or faggot weld to have enough material for the foot.

You can see the extra material or flashing that has to be trimmed off for the finished foot.

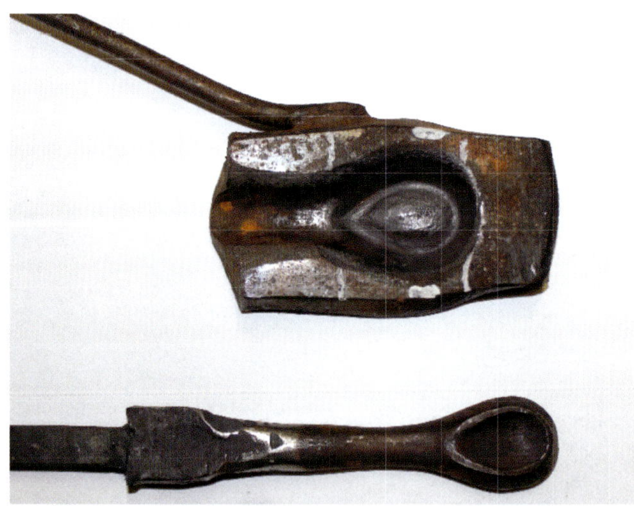

Tool made to create the die.

Foot pressed in bottom die then bent to shape.

Brian Mastropietro
Springfield, Virginia

This is a Eggerling 30 ton press. Originally it was bottom cylinder that Brian had flipped over to make into a top pushing ram.

Quick change combo tooling.

A nice compact cart arrangement.

Brian Mastropietro
Springfield, Virginia

Forging a hawk using the press.

Using a ball peen hammer works well for making a hawk as there is the right amount of material on both ends and the hole is already there so drifting is easy.

Brian uses a series of drifts to drift out the hole to size and shape.

A piece of DOM pipe (Drawn Over Mandrel) is used for its strength and convenience for punching/drifting.

Some hand hammering is still used, but all major material moving is done by using the power of the press. Laying it on its side on an anvil and giving it a few good hits will loosen up the drift.

Christopher Modla
Jessup, Maryland

20 ton horizontal upsetting press that Chris built.

Chris is quite the machinist, engineer, and smith.

This press also raises to vertical and has hydraulic clamps for the work. Limit switches are used to register the depth of consecutive pressings, thereby simplifying repeatable operations.

How do you like this control panel? This is what you can do with solenoids.

Christopher Modla
Jessup, Maryland

The upsetting press in the vertical position.

Christopher Modla Jessup, Maryland

His 28 ton vertical press.

It looks like his mechanicals can power a lot more than this!

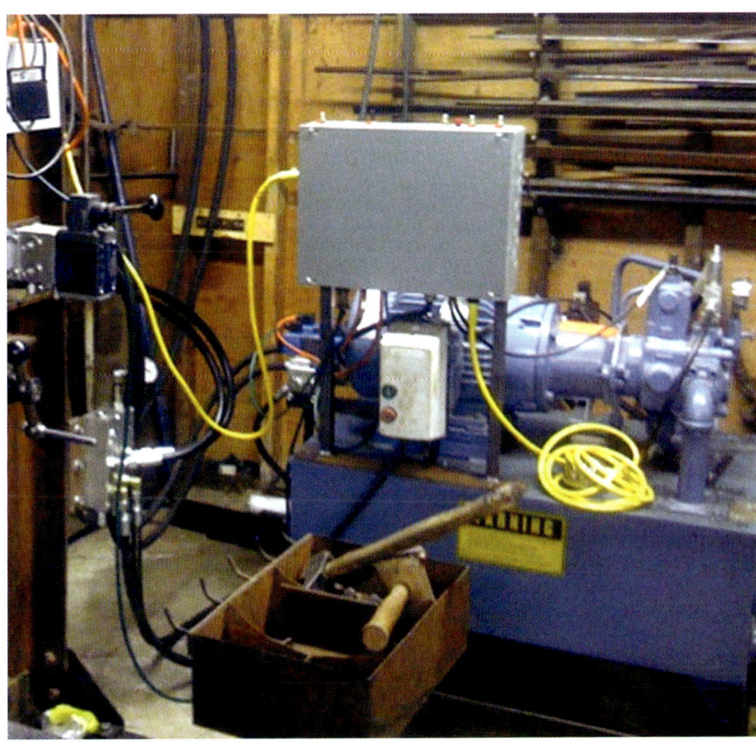

Christopher Modla
Jessup, Maryland

He also uses hydraulics to power this press into the upright position.

And even for a tool clamp and spacing guide on his Kuhn air hammer.

Christopher Modla
Jessup, Maryland

Bending tooling for his press.

Dies and tools, dies CNC milled.

Items made on his press.

Ralph Neumeister
Chagrin Falls, Ohio

Ralph's H-frame 25 ton press.

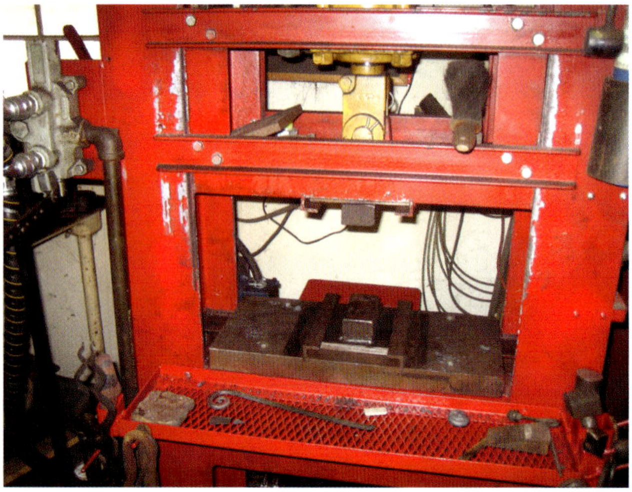

Some of his quick change and handled tooling.

Ralph Neumeister
Chagrin Falls, Ohio

Some of the many items Ralph had made using his press.

Faces using a face die.

Two pieces of I-beam squished.

John Perilloux
Robert, Louisiana

John's 25 ton Claiborne press.

John has had this press for almost ten years. He wishes that he had a foot pedal and is planning to build a second press to lessen the amount of time changing tooling. John has three power hammers, but the press does certain operations more efficiently and with more control. He mainly uses the press for bending, flattening, punching and stamping.

Various tooling John has made for his press.

John Perilloux
Robert, Louisiana

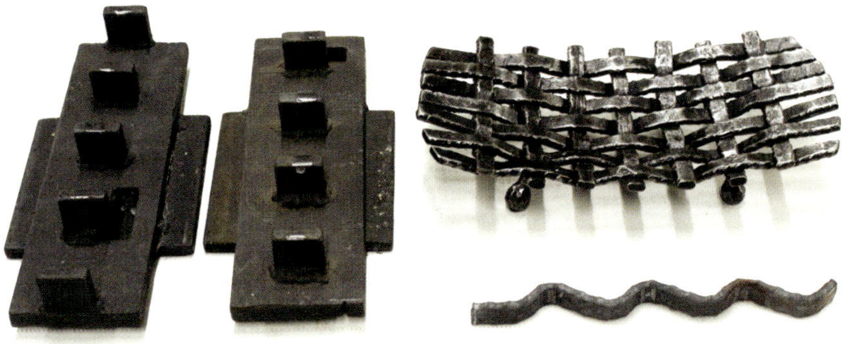

"Tooling that I made to make woven rebar bowls. The corrugation allows me to weave straight bars through the bent bars. After it's woven, the whole piece is pressed flat with die and then shaped."

His press in action using the described tooling.

Tooling to make his business card tray.

John Perilloux
Robert, Louisiana

"I use these to bend heavier stock, hot or cold, such as in this coffee table."

Forged Iron Vine Coffee Table
45"x 24"x18" high
Forged iron coffee table

John Perilloux
Robert, Louisiana

Forged Iron Vine Floor Lamp

This floor lamp shows a base that was made with the lamp base tooling.

Simple tooling to make the floor lamp base.

Bottle opener- slot punch.
This punches from one side only. The slot tooling is raised to allow spacing underneath for the sheared plugs. The plugs have to be cleaned out after about 5 punches so they are not in the way of the next punch.

John Phillips
Montgomery, AL

100 ton industrial press.

Forging a bowl in the press.

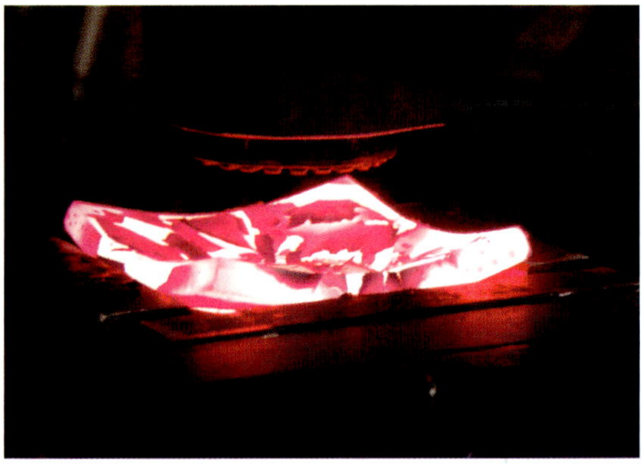

John Phillips
Montgomery, AL

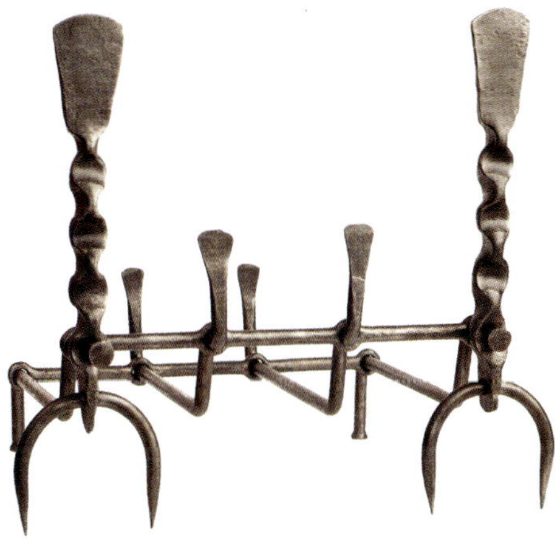

African andirons partially made using the combination fuller.

Top and Bottom Fuller Tool
Made to keep everything square.

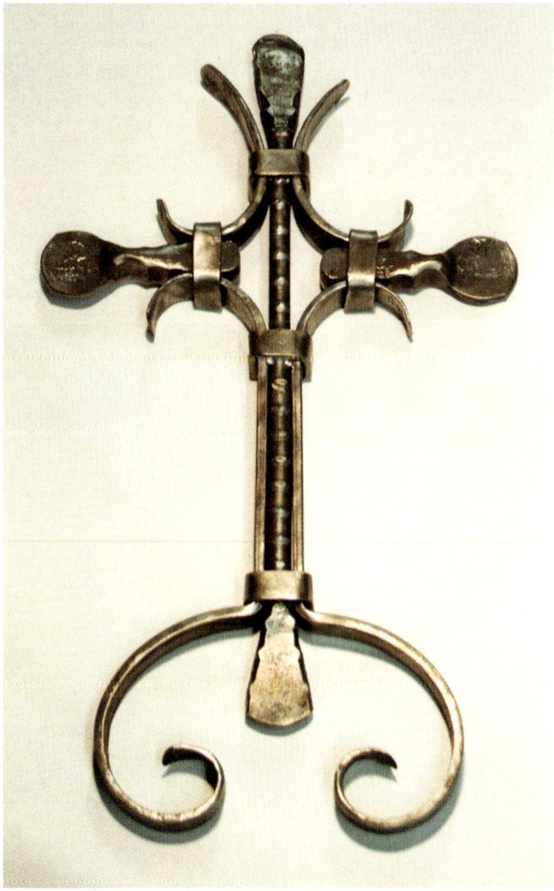

The Cross Regina

The center bar was rebar that was flattened to rectangular leaving the texture on the sides.

Yellin firetool base.
Fullered bar wrapped around plate.

Kevin Potter
Tucson, Arizona

Here are some other photos of the Potter USA 20 ton forging press.

It is 32 inches from the floor to the ram plate so you stand at it in operation.

It is available with right hand or left hand set up and with the tank/motor/pump separate from the press.

Dick Sexstone
Putney, Vermont

20 ton homemade press.

5 inch two way cylinder, 2” shaft, 11” stroke.

Run at 2000 PSI @ 13 gal/min. pump, 11 hp motor. This is run off a log splitter which is outside. This is so quiet the hydraulic fluid can be heard going through the lines!

Dick Sexstone
Putney, Vermont

This shows the foot pedal operation and the linkage that goes to the valve.

Sitting down allows the use of both hands to control your work. It also gives a direct view to what you are doing. It can be operated standing up as well.

Note the hoses tied up and out of the way of heat and rubbing.

The construction of this press was done for precision in its travel. It makes a more accurate job on each push.

Because there is very little slop it is also much more precise concerning the X Y placement of dies.

The view from the chair. You can see the quick change dies and the stops that control thickness of each squeeze.

Dick Sexstone
Putney, Vermont

Cut off is made from H13. There is also a matching top tool. This has held up very well.

Drawing dies. 1”x 1/2” wide.

Squaring or welding die.

Squaring dies for 1” square.

Squaring dies for 1/2” square.

For making V shaped stuff.

Dick Sexstone
Putney, Vermont

The end of a billet welded in the V-dies.

Side view of dies that locate the cabin.

Accuracy- the two sides of a folder ground. Notice where the cabin is located.

Special tooling is required just to position the cabin on the right side of this Damascus handle.

Dies that locate the cabin.

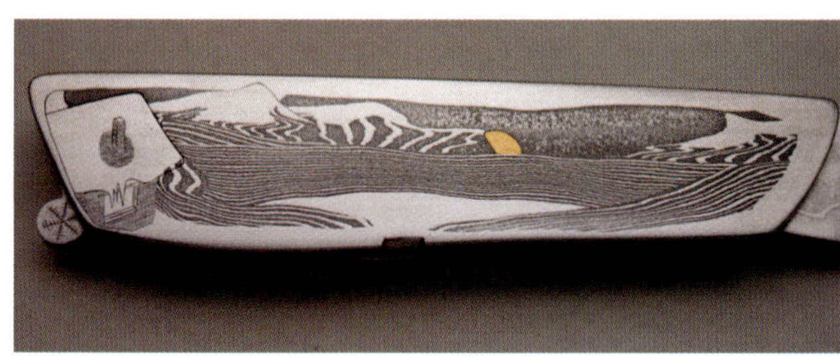

A winter morning. Light is out in the cabin and the sun is risen.

Geese. 15n20 and W2 tool steels.

Dick Sexstone
Putney, Vermont

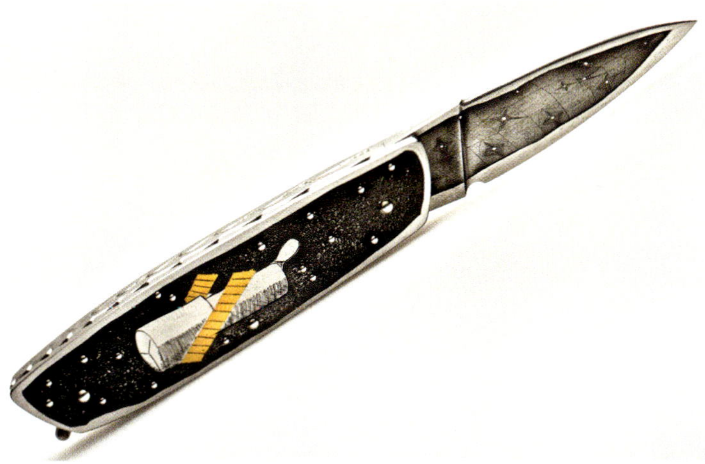

Hubble telescope on this side. Handle: 203E and pure iron. Silver stars, gold inlay.

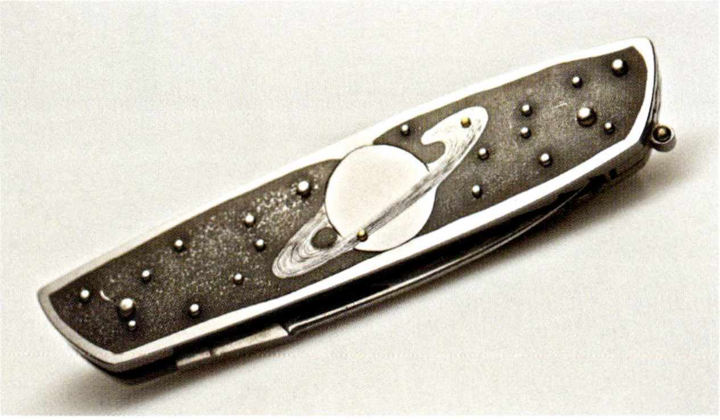

This is other side with Saturn.

Venus & Mars folder.

Stars & Stripes
Blade is 15N20 and 1095 in a flag motif.

Boats are sailing down wind, spinnaker is coming down on the lead boat ready to come about the buoy...

Best things I like abut the press: Control, Control, Control. Its forge welds damascus like a dream.

This is a specialized press for doing knives so there is not much access to the opening. Blacksmithing would require a bigger opening.

TJ Smith
Naches, Washington

20 ton air over hydraulic bottle jack press.

He says it is slow but get the job done for what he needs.

Some knives TJ has made using this press. Some are pressed chain and others are 99 layer Damascus.

Mark Thomas
Markle, Indiana

Toni Thomas at work

Mark uses a modified Uncle Al's H-frame, 24 ton press. He modified it to accept taller dies.

He makes a lot of different types of tent stakes and other items and has created tooling to do it in his press.

Bending Tooling

Bridge Die

James Viste
Hamtramck, Michigan

One of two presses that James uses. This is a C-frame and is about 20 tons.

James uses a combination of stacker blocks. Some solid and others short cuts of I-beam with welded caps to increase their strength to adjust the opening height.

Detail of ram guide.

James Viste
Hamtramck, Michigan

Many of the dies I'm making are done with a fly cutter on the milling machine, the round ones are done this way with the addition of a rotary table.

These are just mild steel untreated and used hot.

Dies and result of the die samples.

I test the die pattern with a crumpled ball of aluminum foil and also how that can be used to emboss copper.

The white test/backing material is a heavy polystyrene that I am still testing.

James Viste
Hamtramck, Michigan

Handled tooling to create his votive candle holders.

Note how the perfect circles are squished into a interesting oval.

Votives 2

James Viste
Hamtramck, Michigan

The press used with simple tooling, a bar, to create an interesting detail in his work.

This is a great example of the press giving the appearance of clay to hot steel!

Squat detail

PLOP - Sake for two, #3

James Viste
Hamtramck, Michigan

Die plate that James created in the middle, the original bar to the right and that bar textured on the left.

Ink well

Two other votive designs.

Votives 3

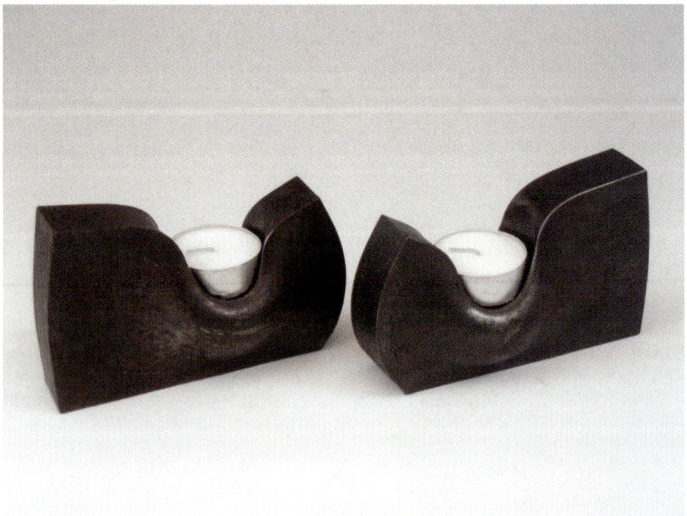

Votives 4

James Viste
Hamtramck, Michigan

More press work

I-beam - 1

I-beam - 2

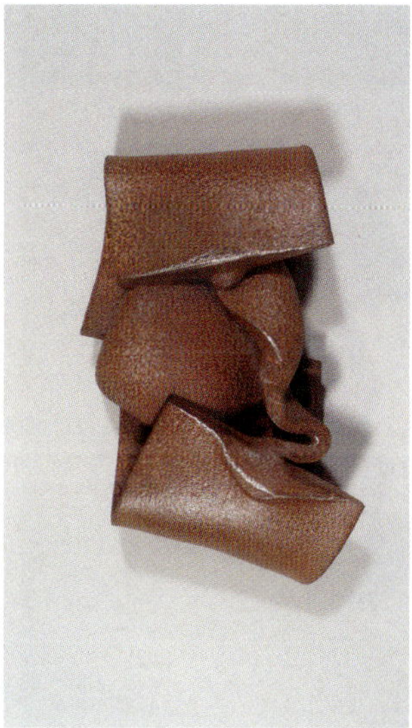

I-beam - 3

I-beam - 4

Bunting detail 2
Part of a gate detail.

Liz Wallace
Santa Fe, New Mexico

Two pendants/brooches using the heart dies with the bottlejack press.

Quilt
Stitched Heart

Sterling silver pressed heart with rare natural Candelaria turquoise. 18 KYG stitching.

Triple Threat
Spiked Heart

Pressed sterling silver heart with spikes and garnet drops.

Summary

This is not everything about forging presses and its tooling. One finds that necessity is the mother of invention and that is where new press designs and new tooling emerge. There are others that use a press for their daily forging and probably have more information to add. Seek them out and see what you can gain from them. I am learning more every day about the versatility of this wonderful piece of equipment.

Hopefully you will have gotten some ideas on how a press will be beneficial to you and your work.

The older I get the more friends are passing on and their knowledge is often going with them. Please find a way to share what you learn through writing, doing videos or giving demonstrations or classes so that we will not have to relearn these skills again. If you can't do this then share with someone who can pass it on. As you learn new ways of using the press or creating new tooling I hope you will share these ideas with the rest of us.

Now I have to get back to the shop and play, I mean learn some more! Have fun! Be safe!

Contact Information of Suppliers and Artist

PRESS MANUFACTURERS

Jeff Carlisle
Great Falls, MT
(406) 590-6181
swain@3rivers.net

Carolina Custom Knives
Tommy McNabb
3217 High Cliffs Road
Pfafftown, NC 27040
(336) 924-6053
www.carolinaknives.com

Ron Claiborne
Knoxville, TN
(865) 660-1569
www.hightemptools.com

Robert Eggerling
29 Oak Road
Mertztown, PA 19537
info@eggerlingdamascus.com
www.eggerlingdamascus.com

Riverside Machine
Al Lawrence
201 W. Stillwill
De Queen, AR 71832
(870) 642-7643
http://w.ivenue.com/riversidemachine

Larry Langdon
Monster Metals
4551 S 192nd Lane
Seattle, WA 98188
larry@monstermetal.org
www.monstermetal.orgPott

Kevin Potter
1934 E. 18th Street
Tucson, AZ 85719
(520) 405-8539
sales@potterusa.com
www.potterusa.com

CONTRIBUTORS, PRESSES & ARTWORK SHOWN

Ron Covell
Covell Creative Metalworking
106 Airport Blvd Ste 105
Freedom, CA 95019
(800) 747-4631
covell@cruzio.com
www.covell.biz

Fabrications Limited
88 Bear Mountain Road
Ringwood, NJ 07456
cscotts1@verizon.net

Antonio Diaz Garcia
Spain
antoniodiaz.art@gmail.com
http://antoniodiazgarcia. com

Steve Gensheimer
24 Meadow Glen Lane
Reading, PA 19607
sgensh@comcast.net

William Greene
Brandywine Forge
201 N 4th Ave # 103
Royersford, PA 19468
www.bvforge.com

Joshua A. Goss
4747 National Western Drive
Denver, CO 80216
info@joshuagoss.com
www.joshuagoss.com

Matt Harris
1760 Principio Furnace
Perryville, MD 21903
harrismetal@aol.com
www.harrismetalsmith.com

Nebojsa Ilijeviv
Milana Blagojevica Spanca 12, 11090 Belgrade, Serbia
neboja@nit-art.com
www.nit-art.com

Bruce Jarrell
305A West Haven Drive
Severna Park, MD 21146
brucejarrell47@gmail.com

Chad Jorgenson
155 N. Main
Ephraim, Utah 84627
chadjorgenson@live.com

David B. Kayne
100 Daniel Ridge Road
Candle, NC 28715
(828) 667-8867
kaynehdwe@charter.net
www.blacksmithdepot.com

John Kimball
370 Moiese Lane
Stevensville. MT 59870
Steelhed1@gmail.com

Brian J. Mastropietro
5402 Danville Street
Springfield, VA 22151
(703) 419-1403
mash8001@cox.net

Randy McDaniel
Artist In Forged Metals
@ExPRESSive Metals
Rams4g@msn.com

Heather McLarty
Los Angeles, California 90042
steelcrazy@roadrunner.com

Christopher Modla
1843 Montevideo Road
Jessup, MD 20794
cmodla@comcast.net

Ralph Neumeister
17231 Messenger Road
Chagrin Falls, Ohio 44023
mtforge@cebridge.net

John Perilloux
John Perilloux Metal Art
P. O. Box 307
Robert, LA 70455
(985) 542-4346
johnperilloux@bellsouth.net
www.johnperilloux.com

John Phillips
313 E. Jefferson Street
Montgomery, AL 36104
(334) 263-9931
john@phillipsmetalworks.com
www.phillipsmetalworks.com

Don Plummer
392 Hallman Mill Road
Phoenixville, PA 19460
PlumDon@aol.com

Dick Sexstone
188 Newman Hill Road
Putney, Vermont 05346
richardsexstone@gmail.com

Ed Small
Rt.1, Box 178-A
Keyser, WV 26726

Thomas J. Smith
110 Wanabee Lane
Naches, WA 98937
blksmith@clearwire.net

Mark Thomas
5391 N-400W
Markle, IN 46770
mark@mtforge.com
www.mtforge.com

James Viste
9745 Dequindre Street
Hamtramck, MI 48212
(313) 587-8899
grumblejunky@hotmail.com

Liz Wallace
PO Box 28132
Santa Fe, NM 87592
meliz57@yahoo.com
www.lizwallacerocks.com

Index

Bold numbers and the letter p denote pictures.

Biography

Randy McDaniel began his experience in forging metals more than forty years ago with a class from an 81-year-old blacksmith in 1972. That was the spark that ignited his passion for forging hot metal. Randy also learned from other "retired" smiths, researching the craft in libraries, by taking craft school classes from various skilled smiths such as Frank Turley, Francis Whitaker and Ivan Bailey, and by participating in blacksmithing conferences. Mr. McDaniel traveled to England in 1987 to participate in the British Artist Blacksmith Association's International Conference in Hereford and to study ironwork in London. In 1988 Randy was baptized as a master-smith by Manfred Bredhol from Aachen, Germany.

Randy has always found great enjoyment in introducing others to this glorious craft. An important part of his blacksmithing experience has been advancing their skills and visions. Randy has taught basic and advanced workshops for more than thirty-five years. These include workshops at the University of the Arts, Philadelphia, PA, Penland School of Crafts, New England School of Metalwork, J.C.Campbell Craft School, Appalachian Center for Crafts, Peters Valley Craft School and for many regional blacksmithing groups nationwide and in Newfoundland, Canada. Randy was also a lecturer and demonstrator for the Artist-Blacksmith Association of North America's International Conference at Alfred, New York in 1990 and at LaCrosse, Wisconsin in 2002.

Originally specializing in Colonial reproduction ironwork taught him the basics of forging hot metal. Randy's blacksmithing experience has included a wide diversity of works that runs the gamut from designing and producing personal and whimsical items from business card holders and furniture to large-scale lighting, gates, grilles, fountains and sculptural pieces. His design and forging of the artwork for the new Children's Garden entrance arbor at Hershey Gardens is an excellent example of his art and whimsy.

Currently Randy specializes in work done with the hydraulic forging press. He has done much to promote the forging press to the blacksmithing community. Randy creates all of his own tooling and dies and loves how the forging press pushes hot metal as if it were clay in his hands. His line of hot forged bronze belt buckles is a much sought after collectable. He is available as an instructor or demonstrator.

Mr. McDaniel has also gained recognition and acclaim for writing and illustrating "A Blacksmithing Primer, A Course In Basic And Intermediate Blacksmithing". Blacksmiths, blacksmithing groups and even schools around the world are using this book to teach basic to intermediate forging. This book has also been professionally filmed as a 6 hour video/DVD with Randy's instruction and demonstration. He has also written articles for "Fabricator Magazine" and "The Anvils' Ring".